E

By Elaine

MW00941386

PURPOSE

When the Holy Spirit of Jesus Christ revealed to me my uniqueness created by Father God, it was the most humbling experience of my life. There is nothing prideful in saying I am special. Those who know me see an open mouth with an insert foot personality. I am not afraid to speak my mind and often times get in trouble doing so.

Since childhood, I knew I was special. Over my lifetime, there has been this knowing sense of being chosen. The very first lesson I learned through a gift of knowledge, is that I am like a snowflake. Not only me, but also we are all like snowflakes, each with their beauty and uniqueness. We are each beautiful and unique to Jesus. Those who are not spiritual minded view those that speak directly to the Holy Spirit as foolish. All I can say is that I have connected to the Spirit of Jesus and I try to follow his direction in life.

As I began to write down the wisdom the Holy Spirit shared with me, I was moved in my spirit as I realized it was not my wisdom but His. Yes, I am special to Him, and yes He shares His wisdom with me because I dared to ask Him. It is a gift from God the Father, through the Holy Spirit in Jesus' name. In other words, I am only special because of Him.

This gift of knowledge is prompting me to share publicly His words. He has given me urgency and told me the time is **now**! Although what I've written is extremely personal to me, I am compelled to offer His message to you. For me not to share what I have been gifted, would be an insult to the Gift-Giver. Holy Spirit wants to reveal Himself to you and also reveal to you things about yourself you have not yet realized. All things considered, the purpose of me sharing my book is to bring honor to the Gift-Giver as He reveals to you, what so ever it is you need to know.

THANKS

The Holy Spirit has carried me through the process. He chose to use me to present to who so ever will read Elaine's Book of Whispered Wisdom. For holding me in my neutral place until just the right moment to release my book I am most grateful. Only the Holy Spirit knows the fruit that will ripen as a result of His blessed gift.

My husband, Jim has encouraged me to pursue publishing. Jim has been prompting me to complete and release my book for several years. Thank you for having the faith in me when I was just resting in neutral.

To my grandson, Gary James a special thank you for all your help in organizing, editing and all that it takes to make this book a reality. Your encouragement and support has been most valuable to me.

DEDICATION:
  With much love and appreciation
this book is dedicated to my family.

INTRODUCTION

I Corinthians 1:26-31
Brothers, think of what you were
when you were called, not many of
you were wise by human standards;
not many were influential; not many
were of noble birth. But God chose
the foolish things of the world to
shame the wise; God chose the weak
things of the world to shame the
strong. He chose the lowly things of
the world and the despised things
and the things that are not-to nullify
the things that are, so that no one
may boast before him. It is because
of him that you are in Christ Jesus,
who has become for us wisdom from
God-that is, our righteousness,
holiness and redemption. Therefore,
as it is written: "Let him who boasts
boast in the Lord."

It is my privilege to have
been chosen by God to present
<u>Elaine's Book of Whispered
Wisdom</u>. By the world's standard, I
am a foolish, weak and lowly
individual. Who in the world would
have chosen someone like me to

write anything the world might stop and read? No one! Yet, I'm here to tell you my God did. His name is Jesus Christ.

At sixty-five years of age-a wife, mother and grandmother, could I be a writer too? Jesus knew I could be. What the world saw was a woman well into her senior years, confined to her wheelchair for the past thirty-six years, with absolutely no higher education or known artistic talent. I was an ordinary mom who cooked meals and did laundry. The world would snicker at the thought that I could be anything more than foolish, weak and lowly. Ah! Jesus knew I could be more. Jesus looked and said, "This is an individual that I can use." Having said that let me make it very clear that what I have written did not come from me, it came from somewhere deep within my being where the Holy Spirit lives. I have merely yielded myself to be the tool in the Master of all wisdom's hand. Credit and praise of any wisdom that the reader absorbs must be given to only God.

Between 2004 and 2007, I spent time writing down these

messages of wisdom making note of the date. Maybe, some of my readers will have a connection to a certain date that holds a special meaning to them. The conversational nature of the writings presented is outside the rules of grammar because that is the way in which I received His message.

It has been several years and I am just now presenting <u>Elaine's Book of Whispered Wisdom</u> publicly. Why did I wait so long to do this? God's timing is very important in the planting of His seed. Until now, I never felt a sure sign to go forward in presenting my book. It has just been now in April 2013 that I have a sense of urgency to get my book out to the public. There is so much happening in the United States and around the world that raises many questions for each of us. Only God, through the power of His Holy Spirit, can guide each person. We ask why and only He has the answer. He directs and guides each as He sees fit, we need to trust and obey as He guides us. It is time for me to encourage you to seek Him out, in the same way He spoke to Adam and

Eve in the Garden of Eden as they walked together in the cool of the day. We all have heard that the Holy Spirit does not change. It is time to embrace this fact and seek Him out with our questions and concerns. He will find a way to answer you, either by His still small voice or some other way that He chooses. There really is no other one we can turn to in these humanly confusing times. Let me encourage you to praise God for who He is and present yourself to Him for His guidance in your life. I speak not of a specific religion, but of a seeking out of the person of Jesus Christ through His, Holy Spirit to bring honor to the Heavenly Father. We each need to envision our self standing before Him, looking into His eyes, boldly in the knowing that in doing so we stand in the righteousness of Jesus Christ. If you are a child of God, it is your inheritance to stand as Jesus stands with all the power and privilege the Father chooses to release to you. If you are not a child of God, let me encourage you to seek Him out and ask Him to reveal to you who Jesus Christ is, the son of the Living God.

Father is spirit who made Himself a body, Jesus Christ through whom the Holy Spirit lived and worked. After the death and resurrection of Jesus Christ, that same Holy Spirit was given to who so ever will believe that Jesus Christ is the risen Son of the Living God. This Holy Spirit lives in all believers to guide and teach us all we need to know to fulfill our individual purpose. Seek Him out and be blessed. He wants your friendship and fellowship at this very important time in history. Do not hold back as He is reaching out to you, His dear child:

Psalms 46:10-11 "Be still and know that I am God.

I will be exalted among the nations;

I will be exalted in the earth.

For me, I sit in prayerful praise in a quiet place. After I have spent some time thinking and praying, on the awesomeness of God I stop and sit still in His Presence. Listen to Him! I simply begin to write what I hear. That small whisper that is deep inside of me. I do not think about what I am hearing, I just write it down. It all happens very quickly. When the voice stops, I'm done. It is as simple as that. My God is not complicated. He will never tell me anything that will go against the Holy Bible. The same small whisper spoke to the ancient prophets too. A lot of what is written seems to be repetitious. I offer no apology for this, as I believe we grow through hearing the same things repeatedly. It is my sincere hope that you who choose to read what I have been privileged to write, will find growth in your own personal relationship with Jesus Christ.

Be Blessed,
Elaine M. Petersen

PREFACE

Seek me early.
Go up to the mountain and seek
my face.
Know that I Am, God almighty.
I Am the beginning and the end.
Honor and Glory belongs to me.
Come with a pure heart.
Put no other gods before me.
Focus on me, the one true God.
I Am the light and the way.
Follow Me.
 - Holy Spirit August 2004

CHAPTERS

CHAPTER 1
Seek Me Early

Genesis 1:1
In the beginning God created the
heavens and the earth.

Genesis 1:27
So God created man in his own
image, in the image of God he
created him; male and female he
created them.

August 2004
Where I Am, you can be also. Be
still. Be my friend.

Yes, Lord I will be your friend.
Teach me how to love you.

Come closer and hear me.

What is it Lord, what do you want
me to know?

I love you with an everlasting love.
Before the foundation of the world
I knew you, and loved you. I
formed you for my purpose.

What is your purpose Lord?

**For my pleasure I created you.
From dust to dust I created you
for my pleasure.**

How do I please you Lord? What is
in me that pleases you?

Your loving kindness pleases me.

Show me how I am loving and kind.

**In that you show love to the least
of mine you show it to me.
Therefore, I love you with
everlasting love.**

September 30, 2004
What do I need to know today, Lord
Jesus?

**I Love you with an everlasting
love.**

Thank you Lord. I know this. What
else do I need to know today?

**Go in my name and in my strength
wherever I send you. Open your
eyes and see. Speak what I give
you. Be gentle as a dove and wise**

**as a fox. Let my Spirit do its work.
Time is short. Work while there is
today. Give no thought for
tomorrow. I take care of today and
tomorrow. Lean on me. I will
strengthen you for the task at
hand. Today is the day the Lord
has made, be glad and rejoice in it.**

Yes Lord, I will take today and let
you live through me. Thank you
Lord.

October 1, 2004
What do you want me to know today
Lord?

**Rest in me. Do not struggle to do
my work. It is not you, but the
Holy Spirit in you that does my
true work. So, sweet daughter, rest
in me. See if I will not speak for
you. See if I will not use your body
as my vessel of clay. Be my vessel
only and let my Spirit speak. Rest
in me. Rest in me. Let my
convicting power flow through
your earthen vessel. I love you
yesterday, today and forever. I will
never leave you. Rest, rest in me
now. I Am, a now God forever and**

**ever and ever. Yield to me. Time is
short and the harvest is ripe. They
will come to you, those who need to
hear what the Spirit has to say.
Time and times are running out.
Gather my wheat, lovely daughter.
I love you as you love me.
Remember, true love is to serve
the unlovely. So be it.**

Thank you Lord.

October 4, 2004
Give me clear direction.

**Pray without ceasing. Honor me in
all you do. This is prayer without
ceasing.**

Thank you Lord for this direction.

October 6, 2004
Show me Jesus in me.

**See if I will not open the windows
of Heaven and show a blessing you
cannot think or imagine.**

What blessing is this Lord?

Jesus in you the hope of Glory. Glory now-for I Am-a now God. Yesterday, today and forever. The Alpha and Omega, from everlasting to everlasting. All knowledge and wisdom are in me. Know that where I AM you can be also.

How do I get there Lord?

Rest in me is the key. Do not strive or struggle. My words will come from you. Out of your belly. Glory and honor are mine to share with whom-so-ever I will. You are not in control of me, I Am in control of you. So rest in me sweet daughter. Rest in me. Your strength will be renewed in me.

Thank you Lord.

October 7, 2004
Jesus, today is a new day. What do you want to tell me?

I have made this day; be glad and rejoice in it.

I am happy and trusting in you this

day Lord.

I bring you before my Father this day. His power is unceasing and mighty. Stand before Him with a pure heart. A heart joined in mine at the throne of the all Mighty One.

Jesus, help me focus on the Father together with you. What else do I need?

Realize His mighty power.

How can I receive this power to accomplish God's will in my life?

Just be the pot. Available and willing. Go when He says go and rest when He says rest. Rest now and trust His word. All knowing and sovereign.

I will continue to trust and rest.

Thank you Lord Jesus.

October 11, 2004
I'm here Lord.

Heart to heart. Father to child.

What Lord?

Father's heart beats with love for child. Be my child and hear my voice, the one who loves you with an everlasting love.

Thank you Father. I am trying to listen.

Do not strive, be who I made you to be. I will give you clear instruction when time is right. Continue to rest and wait on me. All is well now. Continue to praise and trust in me. The sovereign one, the Creator of the universe and all things.

I trust your judgment Lord. Thank you.

October 13, 2004
Give me sound advice.

Hear me oh child. Be not conformed to this world as other men are. Be formed by me. I will mold you into a vessel of honor.

I yield myself totally for your purpose. Help me to hear and see what you say.

Vessel of honor, be prepared, ready in season, for the season is now. Be not afraid but obeying. I will give you strength and knowledge for what you will do in my name and in my might. Be alert and listen with holy ears for my direction and calling. Time is short. Be willing, clean and holy. Be open to my call, it will be very soon. All your children will know me as they witness my great might. Hold fast and be faithful and true. I Am true to my words, you be faithful and true to your word of commitment to me and my purpose. My blessings for you are far above what you think or expect. I love you with everlasting love, from everlasting to everlasting. Be not troubled, I Am faithful and true my faithful daughter. Amen.

Thank you Lord for ears to hear.

October 14, 2004
I have no questions. I praise you for a completed plan.

Vessel of honor, my sweet daughter. How proud I am of you this day. Keep in the light and the glow will shadow (shield/protect) you. Others will see the light and question it's glow.

Thank you Lord. Please help me to stay in and follow your light.

I will light your way. The path you follow will be clear and definite. Hold fast to me, I will not let you go. Together we will pursue this journey. Exciting. I Am as excited as you are to be traveling with you. We will go many places together in power and might. I have chosen the foolish to confound the wise.

In the natural I do not have many talents Lord. I'm depending on you to supply all I need for this journey.

My supply is ample. You need not ask for what you need for it is already in place. It all will come

**very smoothly as the need is
required. My supply is endless.
Stay in the light and it will reflect
naturally from you. My nature is
light and only light. My love is
everlasting and true.**

Thank you my Lord.

October 15, 2004
Lord, you are in charge of the
universe. What do I need to know
today?

**The wind blows where I will, so
my Holy Spirit flows where I will.
Let my Spirit flow through you as
I will. Remember, be the pot only.
I will fill and I will empty where so
ever I will. Be alert, be the pot.**

Thank you Lord. I give over the pot
for your purpose.

**Let the water of my Spirit flow
and empty over the hungry and
thirsty. My supply is endless and
everlasting. See me flow when I
say go. Trust me only for I Am a
jealous God. My beloved of the**

Beloved. I'll be faithful and true. You be faithful and true. Together joined, Spirit to Spirit.

Awesome Lord. Thank you for the encouragement.

You're welcome.

October 19, 2004
Lord, you alone are all knowledge and truth. Share with me.

Come close my child. Rest on my bosom. Hear my heart.

Yes Lord, I know you want me close to your heart. What do you need me to know this day?

You are my heartbeat. Joined together with my Beloved, you also are my beloved. Wait a while longer for clear instruction. Just stay close and continue to hear my voice. Learn to listen to be my voice. The world is waiting to hear what you have to say in my name and in my might. I have not forgotten you. You are being tested and fit for my use. You are doing

**well. Keep going forward and
upward. The higher place is made
ready for you. You will not be
alone for I will never, never leave
you. I see your heart as sincere and
true. Honesty, purity and willing
are in you. Stay in the light,
everything will be all right.**

Thank you Jesus.

October 25, 2004
What is wrong with me that I think I
do not love you enough? Dear Jesus,
be with me as we approach God
Almighty to answer.

**Fitly joined together is love. It
takes two to love, Father and Son;
Son and child. Interacting, giving
and taking. Yielding to and
receiving from.**

Am I doing these things Lord?

**Yes, my child you speak and I
speak back. I direct and you
follow. I'm with you as you follow
clear direction. This pleases me to
know you trust and obey. Keep up**

**the good work. There is much
more to be accomplished in my
might and in my power. Keep
remembering you are just the pot.
My yielded vessel. I will fill and I
will empty. Relax and do not allow
the evil one to tell you that this is
not love. There is nothing selfish
about obedience. This pleases me
when you trust and obey. When
you acknowledge me, as the I Am-
the alpha and omega, the one who
works everything for good to those
that trust and obey. I love you. I
love you. I love you. From before
the foundation of the world. I
knew you and what we together
would accomplish for my
Kingdom.**

Thank you my Lord for loving me.

**From everlasting to everlasting I
love you. Faithful and true I love
you.**

October 29, 2004
Lord Jesus, do you have a special
word for me today?

Be in the light and be my light this

day. Glow and let the after glow of my Spirit do its work. Work for today as the day is short and the night comes soon.

Thank you Lord, give me more wisdom.

Wisdom comes by hearing my word and words. Fear not what you should say. I will provide the correct words for the time and season. Autumn is harvest time. My light is bright for those who are seeking to see it. My words are life to those I am calling. Be alert, hear and speak when I say speak. Do not cast your words before the swine, only the sheep that I am calling. I know all things and the condition of men's hearts. Pray men's hearts be in the right place for me to move by my Spirit. Spirit joins spirit not flesh. Help me to rejoice in gathering of my sheep. Vessels are few and my flock is lost and seeking. Come and call, I want them all.

Thank you Lord. Tune my ears to your sound.

October 31, 2004
Lord Jesus, what word do you have
for your children this day?

**Be still and come close, hear my
words. Focus on me to hear and
see. Time is now to gather my
wheat. Open your eyes and see
those who hunger for me. Hope is
in me, the one who created all
things for my pleasure.**

How will we know them Lord?

**My Spirit in you will know them.
My Spirit in you will speak the
word each needs to hear.
My Spirit will comfort and heal
those who are seeking.
My Spirit will water and prune.
Just be my vessel yielded for my
use.
Be not zealous in your flesh to do
my work.
My Spirit will do my work
through you.
Rest in me and let my Spirit flow.
Harvest time has arrived. Do not
let my wheat be wasted in the
fields.**

**Loving child, obey me.
See me and obey.**

Thank you Lord Jesus. I will try my best to rest and obey.

November 1, 2004
A new day, do you have a plan for me this day?

Join in prayer this day with me and my purpose. Be confident in my plan for this nation. Be not afraid but encouraged, as all things will work together for good to those who love me and are called by me. You are blessed and called. Your prayers in my righteousness avail much. Pray while it is day. Night comes very soon. Your children will be covered and protected from the evil one and his dark doings. Be uplifted and look up to me the Mighty One the Creator of all good things. Be a partaker of my righteousness.

Thank you Lord. Should we prepare for this darkness to come?

**Be concerned of today only.
Tomorrow is not and yesterday is
gone. I will be with you to be your
guide. I will light your path as I
Am the way to all truth and light.
Light into light will guide through
the night. Amen**

Thank you for all you do for me my
Lord and Savior.

November 4, 2004
Take me afresh today. Cover me in
your righteousness and use me for
your purpose.

**Take in my breath of life. Breath
and be at peace. Just be with me
and let me dwell in you. Today is a
day of rest and peace. Just keep
me company.**

Thank you Lord for my peace and
comfort. Do I comfort you also?

November 5, 2004
Lord Jesus, take me and use me this
day. Guide me for your Glory and
purpose.

I Am working to bring heaven to earth. There will be a new and mighty move as I prepare my Saints to fulfill my will on earth. Be ready and alert be not surprised but expecting a great move of my Spirit. I will move on the hearts of men. Be ready to speak what I give you. Be gentle and not overpowering. My Spirit will move and do my work. Be humble as my earthen vessels. Speak truth in love. I Am love divine. I'm looking for men to yield and love me back. You must forsake yourself and your fleshly ambitions, as time is so short. Time of this season will run quickly and the harvest must be brought in before the storm. Rest in and look to me as your guide. As those who travel a journey are in subjection to a tour guide, rest in me and let my Spirit be your guide. I know the places you must go to find the ripe wheat. Follow me, I know where and who they are. Who is hungry will be fed and watered. It is getting late for pruning. I'll take those who hunger and thirst. Let my Spirit be free in your rest and

seek and save those who are the lost. My beloved of the Beloved, hear and see.

Lord Jesus, I am here and willing to do your will. Give me ears to hear and eyes to see what your Spirit is doing.

Rest and tune in dear child.

November 7, 2004
Light the way for my way. Be not afraid but obey, vessel of light in the darkness. People are watching and will see the light. They will be curious and seek you out for answers. You will share what you know as truth that I have taught you. Do not be concerned of what others speak. My Spirit will bear witness to the true truth. Rest and speak what I have given you. Be faithful and true to me as I Am faithful and true to you. Precious child, hear and do as I have taught you, my love, my sweet child. I love you.

Thank you Lord. Teach me of this deep love.

November 8, 2004
Woke up this morning to a voice that
said, "Why?" My question Dear
Lord is, "Why what?"

Why art thou thus?

I do not know Lord why?

**Am I not God? Do I not know all
Things? Have I not made all
heaven and earth? Do I not know
the beginning from the end? Did I
not know you before the
foundation of the earth? Am I not
your Father in Heaven and on
Earth?**

Yes Lord, you are all these. Why did
you say "Why?"

**Just to show you how foolish it is
to question me. I have asked you to
trust me. All things together are
working for your good and for my
purpose.**

I do know this Lord and yet I do
question why your word says we are
healed through Jesus and yet I do not

see the manifestation in my flesh. You say you have not because you ask not, and yet many and I have asked and prayed and believed for my healing. Excuse me Lord, but why do we not see me healed on earth because I do understand this is accomplished in heaven.

Does the one who set the stars in place and balances all that is in heaven and earth know how to balance all things one with the other?

Yes you do Lord. So maybe I should be asking not 'why' but 'when?'

There is an exact moment in time, planned very long ago, when all will be perfectly balanced for my purpose.

OK Lord, I thank you and trust you to complete my healing. But you are going to have to give me whatever it takes to be able to trust you.

I love you and have always supplied all your needs.

CHAPTER 2
Go Up to the Mountain and Seek My
Face.

2 Chronicles 7:14
*If my people, who are called by my
name, will humble themselves and
pray and seek my face and turn from
their wicked ways, then will I hear
from heaven and will forgive their
sin and will heal their land.*

November 10, 2004
Good morning Lord, give me fresh
manna for today.

**Come unto me and I will supply all
your needs. I have all riches and
glory. Your portion is ready and
prepared. Just receive it as you go
from task to task this day. You
need not know what you need.
Your loving Father has already
prepared your portion for when
you need it. Relax and enjoy the
day and let my Spirit lead you.
Flow with my glow, just let my
nature come forth. No need to
struggle, just let go and let God be
God through you. Blessed child, I
love you so you will never know**

**the depths of my love for you, my
faithful and true child. Go now
and remember, let me be God.**

Thank you Lord for the
encouragement. You make it so easy,
yet we try sometimes to make it
complicated.

Rest in me.

November 13, 2004
I'm here Lord, what do you want to
say this day?

**Honor me this day as you do what
I say. Continue to rest and obey.
My love is here to stay.**

Lord, help me to open my heart to
receive all the love you care to share
with me.

**Rest and obey for there is no other
way. Be happy in Jesus as you rest
and obey. Simple truth, simple
task. Just ask and receive as you
rest and obey.**

Thank you Lord. I give myself into
your rest. I open my spiritual eyes

and ears. How do I rest and ask at the same time?

Faith brings rest. Resting in confidence brings healing.

I rest in your completed work. Thank you Lord and Savior.

November 16, 2004
Do you have any advice for today?

Come with me on your journey of life. I Am life, I Am the way. Come along with me sweet daughter. The journey will be pleasant as you rest in confidence that I not only know the way but that I too am the way. Away with me into my secret place. I love you there. I love you here. My love is endless, no boundaries can bind it, nothing can hinder it. My love is now and forever.

Lord, I know you love me in my mind, but I'm having a problem receiving all you are offering me. Show me how to grasp and hold this love as mine. I know I cannot earn it. It is your gift to me.

Relax and receive, receive and let me pour it out to others. This is my plan. The work is completed today is the day.

Lord help me to receive even if I do not completely understand. Thank you my Lord.

November 18, 2004
Here I am Lord. Give me wisdom for today.

Come to my secret place. Dwell in peaceful rest with me. I will supply all your needs because you care for me. Wisdom comes to the wise and prudent. My supply is endless. There is plenty to go around.

Thank you my Lord. Do you have a special word for me today?

I have made this day, be glad and rejoice with me in it. Come up higher to my place of peace that sits above the cares of this world. The place where my blessings are lasting to everlasting; my place of peace and joy as you rest in me.

Things of this world pass away
with time, but in my secret
dwelling place we have peace and
joy forever and ever.

Can you reveal more of your love in
this secret place, my Lord?

Hunger and thirst for my love and
my righteousness. The secret place
holds all the answers, all the
wisdom, all the knowledge that is
mine. I will share as I see fit. Cloth
yourself in all I have and you will
know more of my deep love-deep
into deep. Be not afraid but
trusting. You can do nothing in
yourself. Abide with me my child;
my friendship sticks closer than a
brother. I love you with my
everlasting love I respect you and
your efforts. Relax and be with me,
my love my sweet daughter. I
bring you with me to the Father's
throne of grace this day. Be ready
to receive a special blessing. Take
it in and bless back as you go
forward in my Spirit and in my
strength. Much to do and time is
short. You will speak my words in
due season as the season is now

this very day.

Thank you my Lord, I in faith receive all you care to give me. I'll do my best to follow your Spirit all the days of my life beginning afresh this day. Praise God.

November 19, 2004
Help me.

I will supply all your needs.

Thank you my Lord.

November 26, 2004
Lord, I'm tired in my body. Help me.

I lead you to all wisdom and truth. Rest in me and you will renew your strength. Focus on me, the Creator of you and all things. Relax and rest in me.

Ok Lord, I'm trying to focus and rest in you.

Stop trying and let me do the works. They are finished from the foundation of the earth. Flesh is from earth. Spirit is eternal. Call

**on Spirit to lift spirit. Your body
will follow. Rest and be still. I Am
still Lord. The one who loves you
from everlasting to everlasting.**

Thank you my Lord.

November 30, 2004
What's up?

**Be confident in me. I love you and
gave my life for you. Be still with
me. Come to my secret place.
Peace and tranquility are yours
there. Hold onto me I will never let
you go. Joined together in/by love.**

Help me to know and receive more
of this love you have for me.

December 1, 2004
Lord Jesus, do I understand resting
in you? Give me deeper insight.

**Resting means resting from all
your labors. Take life easy right
now. I will renew your strength.
You can count on me. I Am true to
my word. Rest and gain wisdom
and strength in you body.**

Thank you Lord I'm resting. Why is my body so tired?

You are not resting. Listen to me and rest. I know best.

Why do I feel guilty doing nothing?

You need to listen to me and what I am asking you to do. Rest now. I will make clear your next instruction. Now rest in me.

Okay Lord I'll try harder.

December 3, 2004
Hello Lord I'm here to hear.

Hello yourself. I've been waiting for you to listen. Grace sweet grace. Rest in me. Take comfort in my love for you. You cannot know the depth of my love for you my child. Faithful you are and faithful I will ever be. Your hopes and desires are not too hard for me. Ask much and I will give much. Seek me early and you will find me. My love is everlasting and true love. Deeper than deep and higher than high. Who can comprehend

it? I will teach you more of my love, My Love.

Yes Lord please do. I need to know more of you and your love. I know I cannot know this in my flesh but in my spirit. Fill my hollow place with your love.

Know me, love me, and serve me is my hearts desire for you. I will lead you in all my ways and all of these places. Just continue to trust me and give me access to the pot. I love you a lot. Dear sweet child, just be mine.

Thank you Lord for the visit.

December 10, 2004
Good morning my Lord.

My ways are not your way. My ways are far above what you can think or ask. My ways are best. All for good to those I choose and call. Hear me when I speak and do not be afraid to obey. Blessing and honor from my throne are everlasting blessings. Seek what is everlasting. Seek me and all that is

in me because it is everlasting and will not fade as the flowers and grass fade. You are the splendor of my creation. I Am forming you for my purpose. Pray without ceasing and honor me in all your hand finds to do. I am your strength and your comfort. Seek ye me. I love you my dear child. Go in peace.

Thank you my Lord.

December 13, 2004
Speak to me my Lord.

Grace and mercy are yours this day. Grace to speak what I give you and mercy that I have shown to you, you can show toward others. Time is now. Do not waste the moment. Be alert and pay attention to my Spirit. The Spirit of mercy and grace that must be revealed now.

Where will I go to show this mercy and grace, my Lord?

No special place-every place you go this day. Your light will shine in darkness as you go about your

daily business. Be not anxious but know I Am in you and I will shine in the darkness. Darkness has no place when my light shines.

Yes, my Lord, I know it is you in and through me that shines the light.

You, my child, can do nothing of yourself. It is my Spirit that has done and is doing all my works. Again, relax and just be the pot. Lots to do and time is very short now. My Spirit is calling my vessels of honor to trust and obedience NOW. Vessel of honor, be not afraid but trust in me. I love you forever more. Peace.

Thank you my Lord

December 14, 2004
Here I am my Lord, use me.

Sweet vessel of honor, I do use you. When you go about your daily tasks I am using you as you do all to glorify me. Menial tasks done to my glory are mighty works. Remember, my ways are different from your ways. Be and do what I

have created you to do. You are
my work and my pleasure.

What else should I be expecting in
this earthly life?

So much to be accomplished in
such a short time, more than you
need to know. Take today and live
in today. Tomorrow will be
another NOW. All is working out
as I have planned from the
foundation of the earth. All is on
time and time is running out. Just
be what you were created to be
and leave the rest to me as you rest
in me. Sabbath day-night comes
quickly. Give no thought for
tomorrow. Provision is for today.
Like manna, your portion will
come fresh each day. Days are
short now. Come with me as I lead
you along. I see your heart; I need
you to see my heart. You are what
makes my heart beat. Hear it
pound. Make your joyful sound
back to me. I'll meet you in joyful
praise to me. Renewed and
energized by my Spirit we together
do the true works of praise to God

Almighty.

Thank you my Lord; be with me this
day.

CHAPTER 3
Know That I Am, God Almighty.

Job 11:7-9
Can you fathom the mysteries of
God? Can you probe the limits of the
Almighty? They are deeper than the
depths of the grave-what can you
know? Their measure is longer than
the earth and wider than the sea.

December 15, 2004
Help me my Lord this day.

You know not what to pray for
this day. Fear not, your father in
heaven knows your needs this day.
He has already made provision for
this day. Go in peace and know
that I Am Lord, God Almighty.
Creator of all that is, the good and
what you call bad. But remember
always, Dear Child, all is working
for your good, the chosen of my
creation. Be not afraid but
trusting. All is well with your soul.

Thank you my Lord for peace and
comfort.

My peace is given to you liberally. Recognize it and be grateful for it. You will and are doing mighty things in my strength. All gifts are from me, the one who is above and beneath all that is and will be. Be confident in me, seek me and you will find me every time. I love you with everlasting love. Do not fear what others try to do to you. I will work it all out for good and my purpose. I Am God. You are the created in my image. Reflect me. Let me do the working of it through you. That is my job not your job. Rest in me, and my finished work. Peace be still, I love you.

My awesome Lord, thank you again.

December 19, 2004
Good morning Lord. What's up for today?

Holy child covered with my Son's blood, do not fear this day, I Am with you again and always to light your path. Just follow and be not afraid. No one can harm you or separate you from my everlasting

love. Come let us walk together this path of life. Your life is in me, and all we will accomplish together. Come; come with me.

Yes, my Lord I'm willing to go with you wherever you lead me.

The pathway has been established and we must not vary from it for my purpose to be fulfilled. I will cover and protect you as we travel along. Men will marvel at your wisdom. It is not the wisdom of men but the wisdom of God Almighty. Wisdom all will understand who seek me. Wisdom that is so simple it will confound the wise and prudent. Wisdom that is accepted by my children. You are my sweet child. Do not forget this. You are mine; mine to do with for my pleasure. Continue to seek me and my purpose, rest in me, see if I do not open the heavens for you. More than you can ask, think or imagine. It is my pleasure to do this for you, my sweet child. My love for you is so far and deep and above anything that the human mind can

**comprehend. I love you always
and forever lasting, my sweet love
of the Beloved. Trust in me only.
See my hand lift and strengthen
your mortal body. Soon, I say
soon, my word is true and my
word is my word. Now, go and see
my work this day sweet love my
child.**

Thank you Lord. I accept and release
all you have for me to do in and
through me.

December 29, 2004
My Lord, please help renew my
strength.

**I Am high and lifted up. My holy
train fills my temple. I alone am
the Holy one of Israel. Honor me
and my Majesty. Look to me and
see I Am the only faithful and true
provider of all you need or think.
Do not be ashamed to come to me
in your weakness. I will renew
your strength. Look to and praise
me only.**

Yes my Lord, thank you for all you
are. Have mercy on me.

**Be not ashamed but renewed by
me. I will lift you up to higher
places. Come and rest in me and
my holiness. Glory and honor
belong to me, you can do nothing
of yourself.**

Thank you My Lord.

January 4, 2005
Here I am Lord, can you use me
today?

**Are you available? Come with me
today, come and pray this day.
Together we can accomplish much.
Come and pray and praise my
name. I Am above all that is. All is
mine and I do what is pleasing to
me. Man cannot understand my
ways as they are far above his
thinking. All is working for good
and for my pleasure.**

Yes, my Lord, I know this but it is
hard to understand.

**I do not call you to understand all
things. I call you to come and obey,
to trust me with all you do and**

watch me work it all out for my good and my purpose. You do not have the capacity to understand in yourself. I will give you understanding by the measure you need, no more no less. I know all things and you only see through a glass that does not show you everything. Do not judge anyone or anything I am working with. I only know all things and how everything fits together for my purpose. Focus on me always and you will not go wrong. Come and focus on me and I will supply all your needs. What you want is not what you need. All you need will be supplied daily. Trust Me, the Holy One, the All-Knowing One, the One who loves you now and forever more. My love, my child, listen to my words and obey.

Yes my Lord.

January 7, 2005
Here I am Lord.

Together we stand this day before the Father. He sits above all. Higher than high. He knows all,

**honor belongs to Him, the Most
High God. The one and only true
God of the universe. He has
created all things for His pleasure
and glory. Honor Him, seek the
Son to bring honor and glory to
the Father. The Holy Spirit in you
together with the righteousness of
Jesus works together in all things
to please the Father. Praise ye Him
and Him only.**

Help me my Lord to focus on Jesus
and not on myself. Do not allow me
to make my desires or myself a god.

**Fear not, my child I will be your
constant help in time of need.**

Thanks for your words my Lord.

January 10, 2005
Here I am my Lord, teach me what I
need for today.

**Let us go together to the Father to
hear what we need today. Come, I
say come and sit on my lap in my
throne room. Let me hold you and
protect you for today and for times
to come. Do not forget this day and**

this time, as I protect you this day
so I will protect you in days to
come. All is not well in this world
but in my kingdom all is well and
precisely on time. Be alert and
watch with me. Pray for my
kingdom to come. It is at the
threshold now. Soon you will step
over into another place in my
kingdom. A place of honor
reserved just for you. Each one
who is listening will find his special
place. A place of rest and joy in me
in my kingdom. See what I say,
listen to my voice. The Holy one
the Almighty one. I have a plan
and a purpose in all that I do, have
done and will do. Trust me,
worship me while it is day and
worship me as night is falling
quickly. Be not afraid but trusting.
I Am with you always-now and
forever and ever. I see you, do you
see me and what I Am doing?
Trust me, you do not need to know
everything. Only what I see fit to
show you. Be strong in Faith. Be
spontaneous in season. Be
available when I need you. Keep
me company as I weep for the
world of lost sinners. I need your

comfort too. I have deep feelings of both sadness and joy. I allow what needs be done to bring sinners to there knees. Time runs quickly now as I bring closure to my work. You need not understand all now. You will know as I know soon enough. I love you. Keep in prayer in the Spirit as what you are praying for is a secret to you, only I know all things. I Am trusting you to pray, you can trust me with all that is hidden from you now. So be it.

Thank you my Lord for the privilege to pray.

January 12, 2005
Here I am my Lord.

Be with me and pray this day. Time is ticking, it goes swiftly now. Be aware be alert, my will be done not thyne.

Yes Lord I understand time is very short. Is there a special job or place for me?

You are in your correct place to

hear and pray. I need those who will pray with me.

Thank you my Lord, I pray and trust you to do.

January 12, 2005
Give me truth my Lord.

You are covered by my blood, my righteousness is over you. You can do all things through Jesus Christ who strengthens you. In His power and might all is accomplished for his kingdom.

Yes, my Lord, I know that without you I can do nothing.

Be confident in my strength and in my knowledge. Do not try to draw from your flesh as it is weak and frail. In me and my Holy Spirit you can accomplish what I have set before you. Pray and seek me this is the key. Do not seek out a problem. Seek out me, I only can direct you in the path you must travel. I will lead you, follow and obey. Do not try to work wonders in your flesh. I will direct and I

will give clear instruction, follow me only. Be available for my purpose. Many are seeking to work in the flesh. No! No! That will not accomplish my work. My work is complete. I just need the vessel to pour into that you may pour out when I direct you. Be careful not to go before me. I must go before you. Listen sweet daughter with well-tuned ears. See what I need you to do, be careful.

Thank you my Lord. Please help me to keep my place.

January 15, 2005
Speak, my Lord, I am here.

My child, come to me. Keep it simple. Be clothed in the righteousness of my Son, Jesus Christ. Give yourself a fresh each day. Just be there to help me pray. The world is lost and needs to hear what the Spirit has to say this day. Be faithful and true to me only. I will guide you as I have said before for my purpose. I know your needs and your desires trust me only. I know what is best for you, as I

**know all things, from the
beginning to the end.**

I trust you Lord and give you
permission to do what is best for you
and your kingdom.

**Praise me, praise me-I share my
glory and honor with no other one.
I Am all; I Am wisdom; I Am
truth. You can depend on me. Do
not even think about trusting in
man, as he is weak. Give me your
all. I love you and I only know
what you need. Be with me as I
Am with you always and I will
never leave you. Come to me in
your weaknesses and I will supply
your strength. I have all you need.
I Am all you need. Glory and
Honor are mine. Rest in me and
my finished work. You need 100%
confidence in me. When you are
weary, stop and see me for who I
Am. Lord Almighty. Take care to
focus on me always.**

Thank you my Lord for your words.

January 20, 2005

Thank you for your Word this day.
Please speak to me in your spoken
word just for me.

**Come little child resting and
trusting in me will bring much
comfort and security. You must be
dependent on me and my strength
as we go forward. Each day
remember where your strength is.
It is in my strength. You will do
great things in my strength.
Things that you may not recognize
as great are great to me and my
purpose. Be confident of my
leading you by my Holy Spirit. I
love you and am not willing that
you should be harmed. I Am your
protection as you are covered in
my blood and yielded for my
purpose. Do not rely on the
feelings of your flesh. Spirit leads
Spirit in all truth and goodness.
Come with me, I know the way.**

Thank you my Lord.

January 25, 2005
Talk to me my Lord I'm listening.

Come up, come up to my lap. Let

me hold you and love you this day. Be comforted by your Father in Heaven. I Am holding you tightly to my bosom. Fear not, but have faith in me only, pure childlike faith. Know me and my Word. Be diligent in your reading of my written Word. I will teach you and give new insight by my Holy Spirit. The knowledge that comes from me that you need will be made clear to you. I will and am dealing with you in all things to bring all things together for my purpose. Be true to me in confidence of my knowledge and wisdom. Be not anxious to share all with everyone. Share with Jim as I nurture him through you. You are one with Jim as I Am one with you. Share with Jim his ears are open now and ready to receive. Praise me. I alone am worthy of all your praise. I alone am due all honor and glory. Glorify me as you read and pray for understanding. I alone know your true needs. Desires are being taken into consideration for my purpose and my master plan. I Am Master of all that is. Good and bad are in my control. I only can make

good come forth out of what you call bad. Be faithful to me only. Do not make idols. Do not judge or look at the bad. Look to me for all works for my good and my purpose. Sometimes I need to make use of the bad to bring into captivity the good. Set my people free. Pray with me and move only in my Spirit and strength. Rest and know that the work is done. You need only to obey my Holy Spirit as he reveals what you need to do in my Spirit and might. Be trusting of me I will never fail you or my purpose. Be alert and hear when I speak to you. Yielded vessel of pure gold and honor. Hear me only as I speak to you. I love you with true and everlasting love.

Thank you My Lord I am doing my best. I am so blessed by you. Thank you.

January 26, 2005
I'm praising you this day my Lord.
All is well with my soul.

Praising Me, Praising Me is the proper way to come and see. Seek

**me in your praise. Seek and pray
without ceasing. I Am listening
with great pleasure. You were
created by me for my pleasure. My
greatest pleasure is to hear your
Praises. Understand I Am working
all things together for my purpose.
Trust me, as I know exactly what I
Am doing. Follow me by my Spirit.
Clear direction will come as you
Praise me and my perfect plan.**

Praise you my Lord. What is my
assignment today?

**Praise, Praise, Praise for my
perfect work is complete.**

Thank you, Praise you my Lord.

January 31, 2005
Teach me my Lord, what I need to
know. I need knowledge and
wisdom.

**Knowledge and wisdom are mine
to share as I see fit. Do not worry,
I will be your school master. Open
the books and I will instruct you
by my Spirit. The Spirit of truth
and wisdom. When I say speak-**

speak, when I say be silent-be silent, when I say teach-teach. Let me be in control. You are doing fine. You are right on time. My plan is perfect and all you do in me in my strength, knowledge and wisdom will be perfect.

Thank you my Lord. You are good to me. I appreciate it.

Relax, I will give you all the strength you need to complete my works. Stay in the company of like minded people. You will hold up and support each other. Do not be afraid but trusting. I have all you need and all they need. Make room for human error. Be forgiving and understanding. You are all a work in progress. My will, will be done on earth as it is in heaven. Just come and stay with me. We need each other. More will be explained to you later. Just keep it simple and stay with me. Seek me early each day, I Am there and will never leave or forsake you. Seek and know that I Am with you always sweet daughter. Go in peace this day and listen for me. I

will instruct as you go about the day in and with me. I love you with everlasting love. Amen.

Thank you my Lord.

February 2, 2005
My Lord, please give me clear direction.

You worry too much. I have asked you to trust me. If you need to ask for direction, you are not trusting me. Get back to trusting me and be anxious for nothing. I Am holding you up in all you do.

Thank you Lord. I will trust you. I again give you permission to use this vessel for your purpose.

I'll take it. You have been refined into a vessel of pure gold-my vessel of honor and grace. I give it to you freely and abundantly. Where you go you will be recognized as mine. Be ready to answer them for my glory. I will give you words to say. Trust me. I will never fail you. Your words-I put in you-will accomplish what I have designed.

You will do your part for my kingdom. Let go and let me finish the works. I Am God. Not you or any other vessel. I do give you power at a specific time for a specific purpose. Do not try to figure me out. My ways are different from your ways. My ways will accomplish what I have sent it forth to do. I Am perfect and precise. Praise me for that and trust in my judgments.

I'm praising and trusting you my Lord.

CHAPTER 4
I Am, the Beginning and the End.

Revelation 21:6&7
He said to me: "It is done. I am the
Alpha and Omega, the Beginning
and the End. To him who is thirsty I
will give to drink without cost from
the spring of the water of life. He
who overcomes will inherit all this,
and I will be his God and he will be
my son"

February 4, 2005
I am trusting and submitting my
vessel to you this day My Lord.

**Thank you Elaine. I'll use you as I
see fit this day. Be very alert as my
instructions will be clear and
precise this day-go about your
daily chores and I will let you
know all you need to do for Me
this day. Honor and Glory are
mine, do not think yourself higher
than you are-you are earthen, I
Am the Holy One. The One from
everlasting to everlasting. I share
My Glory with no one.**

My Lord, sometimes you tell me you

share your Glory and Honor with whom you will but today you say you share with no one. Please explain.

Am I not God Almighty who knows all things? Let me be God, you need not know all things.

Okay, thank you My Lord.

February 7, 2005
Thank you for this day My Lord.

You have it. Praise me for all things today. Your needs have been met-rejoice-all else will be added unto you. Praise me and see the wonder of my mighty hand on you. I hear you in the morning. I hear you in the evening.

Tell me more my Lord.

Open your eyes and see my splendor all around you. In my creation in the wonders of nature in the heaven above, in the grass and flowers of the field. All is diverse and splendid for my pleasure. Take time to see my

hand in all I have created. The beauty and majesty of it all. Perfect order and balance. Oh if my creation in man would only yield to me. I wait and weep for such a day when all my creation of man will see me. All will some day see me and kneel and praise me. I wish all would come to repentance before time is spent. Be alert and ready to help me gather them into my bosom. I long to hold and cress them, but I cannot because of there uncleanness. Help me and stay alert as I need you to help me gather them in. Those who are lost and dieing, a perverted generation. Oh how I weep for the them and they do not hear me. Be my voice. The one calling and crying in the wilderness of humanity. Be not ashamed of my words I give to you to speak. Powerful words, anointed by my Holy Spirit. Words of truth and full of life. They will know it is Me, pray that there hearing be not dimmed by there flesh. Speak gently with authority and my blessing. My blessing is on you, my golden vessel of honor. Do not let your

**flesh forbid my lost sheep. If I Am
with you my words will accomplish
that which I have purposed.**

Thank you my Lord. Help me die to
my flesh this day and accomplish all
you have set before me.

February 10, 2005
Cover me completely with your
blood sweet Jesus. Give me truth and
wisdom.

**Yes, come to me in the
righteousness of my beloved Jesus.
You too are my beloved in the
beloved. He in you is your hope.**

Thank you.

**Trust me in all things you set your
hand to do. The doing of it is your
place. The strength and blessing
comes from above in me your
Father. I will strengthen you as
you come to me in faith believing
that all is being done for my
pleasure. Love me and trust in my
judgment. All is working together
for your good and my pleasure.
Keep trusting in me the God**

Almighty of Heaven and Earth. You do not know and understand all things as I do. So just trust in the one who knows all. Rest in me. Carry no unnecessary burden as this is not pleasing in my sight and it serves no useful purpose. It only hinders my work. The work that has been completed must come forth in these final days and times. I the Lord have spoken it and it will come to pass as I Am faithful to my word.

Thank you my Lord.

February 14, 2005
Thank you my Lord for all you do for me. Teach me today for your purpose.

Hold my hand sweet child. Come with me as we visit with the Father this day. He is proud and pleased that we have come together. He is inviting you to sit with me at His throne. Just be still and wait on Him as a child waits for the gift of the Father. He waits also for the perfect time. Draw near and be still before Him. When He speaks

and calls your name be ready to receive whatever He has for you. Special child He has not forgotten you and your faithfulness. Keep in prayer and praise. Know all is working out for His purpose and plan for you. It is perfect for you and you will understand it all bye and bye. The heavenly host watches and waits in excited expectation. They too watch and pray and praise His Holiness. The Highest of the High has his gentle hand on you in this life. A life without end you are ever in His presence and in His divine care. Be not perplexed just trust and obey. All is well with your soul. Amen.

Thank you my Lord.

February 16, 2005
Thank you my Lord for the sunshine and all the little things you do.

Come again to me dear child. Little children know me. Simple trust and confidence in who I Am. Everything sits in the palm of my hand. All has been done and is in my hand. My hand is open not closed. You will receive from my hand what is prepared for you and my purpose. Do not be anxious be my confident little child in simple faith believing that all you are and all you will be rests now in the palm of my hand. You rest in this knowledge I continue to show you. Rest in confidence that I am true to my word. Know that I cannot do otherwise. What I purpose will come to pass. Rest in confidence in me. Look to me and praise and pray to me and who I Am, the One Holy Mighty Creator of the universe. You are important to me and a vital part of my Master Plan. I Am your Savior, Redeemer, Creator, Lover and all and all of everything that is and will be. Mighty and true. I love you from everlasting to everlasting. Rest in my confidence that I will share with you. How strong is that?

Thank you my Lord.

February 18, 2005
Teach me my Lord for your Glory and purpose.

Be still and know me and my purpose. For my pleasure, for my own pleasure you are here. Hear me when I speak to you early in the morning and late at night. Hear my words and direction and obey me. Glory and honor are mine and I will share as I see fit. Honor me in all you set your hand to do. I Am with you to strengthen you and bless the work or your hands. All is for me and my pleasure. You please me, my child. That is your purpose. Be not afraid or anxious. I see all things and I know all things from the beginning to the end. All is well and all you pray for will be accomplished. Time.

What about time my Lord? How do you see time?

Time is my measure. My way of weighing and balancing all that is done. My time and my ways are different from yours. You just leave all to Me and trust Me and My judgment. All is well with your soul.

Thank you my Lord.

February 22, 2005
Teach me truth this day my Lord.

I Am leading you by my Spirit this day as we seek wisdom and truth at the Father's throne. Be not dismayed as you will gain clear knowledge and direction. Go in faith believing I Am always with you and always at your side to guide your lips to speak truth in love for my glory, to enhance my own kingdom and to minister to my own people. My Spirit will bear witness to them and comfort them at there need. Be ready and let me use you. Let the words I give you flow from your lips. They will know it is from me. Glory and honor are mine only. Do not struggle just relax and let my Spirit flow and accomplish my goals. I know all things from the beginning to the end and my words are perfect for every situation and need.

Thank you my Lord, here I am use me this day.

Sufficient are the needs of this day. I hold all the tools and answers for this day. Do not worry about results. Just be willing as a tool in my hand. Thank you for being available.

Blessings are yours and Glory is for you my Lord.

February 26, 2005
Here I am my Lord, send me and teach me this day.

I weigh and balance all things in the human spirit for my good and my pleasure as I weigh and balance all that is in the universe for my pleasure. I Am able to move heaven and earth for my purpose. Be still and know that I the Mighty One true God can and am doing this. Time is my measure. Watch and see my mighty hand at work. Pay attention in the power of my Holy Spirit to discern my hand and all I do. Harsh actions are required now to get the attention of those who are being called in, in these

**last times. Be not disturbed by
what you will see. All is part of a
bigger plan for my purpose.**

Yes my Lord I can sense these
things. What should I be doing?

**Rest and wait on me, pray and
praise the working out of my plan.
You will be asked to speak for me
and I will give proper
understanding when you are
called. Read and gain knowledge
and wisdom. Be not dismayed-
rejoice in the working of my hand
on you. You are a special vessel for
my Holy use. Be available, be the
clay that I have formed and
reformed as needed. You can do
nothing of and by yourself. Be
available when I call. You will
know the correct time and season.
It is harvest time and the crop is
ready. Stay alert my love, the
beloved of the beloved.**

Thank you my Lord.

February 27, 2005
Do you have a fresh work for me this
day?

I Am the light and the way. The light on your pathway. The pathway of life and love everlasting. Follow the light as I Am in and I Am the light. Do not be dismayed as my light is bright and my pathways are clear to those who seek me only. My beloved child, stay in my light as I lead you in your path of life and love. All is well.

Thank you my Lord.

Rest in my confidence. Praise the bringing in of my sheep. Your children will be marching into my fold soon. They will be part of my great and chosen army for these last days. You will march and reap together as you are sent forward for these last times. The wheat is coming in and the prodigals will lead the flock. They will be at the front lines leading the fold toward life everlasting in my bright and holy light. In a land you know not now, that is flowing with milk and honey. Oh how I will rejoice at there coming in.

Praise you my Lord.

March 2, 2005
My Lord, what is your word for me
this day.

**Come and stay with me this day.
We will pray and praise the master
plan of the Father. A plan perfect
in all areas. Who can know the
height and depth of all the wisdom
and knowledge of God Almighty
and Holy? You will know as He
knows as the need arises. Be not
troubled but trusting in all He has
done and is doing. It is not for you
to know all now. Just trust in Him
as He knows your needs each day.
Like manna in the wilderness.
Trust Him to supply you.**

Thank you my Lord for this word.

March 9, 2005
Dear Jesus, what is going to happen
to the United States of America?

**There will be a rising up of good
and evil. Both will be working for
my purpose. Please pray with me**

that all that needs doing will come quickly for the better interest of my own people. Those who know me will hear my voice. They need to take heed to be precisely obedient to my words. Clear instruction will be given. Do not look to your left or to your right. Hear my call and instruction to you. Be diligent to do all I ask of you. If my people will hear my voice and obey my instruction, I will come quickly. Failure to obey will only prolong what needs to be accomplished. The plan is Mine and my Father's, we will do what is necessary to bring all to a climax.

Thank you my Lord. Do you have precise orders for me at this time?

You are where you need to be. Keep listening to me. Know I Am with you and am your very present help in your time of need. All is well and right on schedule. I love you my obedient child.

Thank you my Lord.

March 10, 2005
Speak to me my Lord, I am here to hear.

Take my hand the one that has all in it. Your supply is there and all your needs are met. Where I go you must follow. Some places will seem dark but they are not. Light comes out of darkness. Hold my hand tightly and be not afraid. I will be with you to give wisdom.

Thank you my Lord I knew I could count on you.

Do not push or pull stay strong and steady on your pathway. Remember, I light the way. Hold onto me and the light on the pathway will be clear. One step at a time. Forward toward My perfect will. If I Am for you, I Am also for those of your household. I have confidence in what I Am working out. My confidence is pure and true. I love you sweet child.

Thank you my Lord.

March 24, 2005
Here I am my Lord.

**Yes my sweet child here I Am also.
I Am pleased you have come to me
this morning. My heart is full of
joy. We need to pray together this
day for lost souls. I hear your plea
for my mercy and grace. I Am
moving by my Spirit toward those
who are seeking truth. They will
know my truth and recognize the
lies of the enemy. They will choose
truth in time. Be not impatient
with them as they set their flesh to
one side and seek me. These things
take time. I Am patient and loving
and will carry them through even
when they do not know me. The
faithful prayers of the righteous
avail much. Prayers are strong and
will accomplish that which I
desire. Be faithful to your prayer
life. I Am yoked to you as we pray
for them together.**

Thank you my Lord for you surely
are faithful and true.

**Yes, I cannot be anything else. I
Am Love, unconditional. I will do**

what my word and words have spoken. There is no turning back for Me. I will accomplish what I say. Have faith in Me and My Word. Amen.

Thank you my Lord.

March 29, 2005
Thank you my Jesus for all you do and are doing for me and my family.

I Am here, I Am here do not make space or time for fear. My love is sure and true. It is purer than pure. Deeper than deep. Higher than high. All is well, my plan and purpose will be fulfilled.

I know and trust this to be so my Lord.

CHAPTER 5
Honor and Glory Belongs to Me.

Psalms 8:3-5
When I consider your heavens, the
work of your fingers, the moon and
the stars, which you have set in
place, what is man that you are
mindful of him, the son of man that
you care for him? You made him a
little lower than the heavenly beings
and crowned him with glory and
honor.

March 29, 2005
It is in man to know my ways. I
have written on each heart my
ways. Each man I have given free
will to choose my way written on
his heart or to follow his own way.
Pray that man would be convicted
by what I have written on his
heart. That he would then chose to
follow that Godly conviction. Pray
that I would give him strength for
each day and that man's
circumstances would have him
seek out my strength. Pray man
would recognize where he gets his
strength. He will then bow down
and worship me, the I Am.

April 4, 2005
Hello my Lord. Do you have a word of encouragement for me this morning?

Hello, you too. My sweet daughter my sweet friend. Today is another day I have made, let us just rejoice and enjoy it together. No work to do today, for everything is complete in me. Just relax and praise us. Your family is being called in, my lost sheep my prodigals. They are aware of my calling them. The clay is being softened. I will be reforming my clay into vessels of pure gold. They will be vessels filled for my use in these last days. Days of much darkness are coming to this earth and my light will shine in the darkness. Look to the light. Speak of the light. Do not give attention and glory to darkness. Light will prevail and those who are seeking me will find me as I have spoken. Crossover to my light lost sheep, I Am waiting for you to come. Remember to follow closely my clear instructions to bring my

sheep to me quickly. Not to follow slows down my plan and process. Praise me now and be alert. Peace be with you and my Spirit that is working through you. My faith I give to you freely. Use it for my purpose and my glory. Let my mercy and kindness flow to my lost sheep through my sweet and faithful vessel of honor. Pray and praise moves mountains of darkness. The enemy has to flee from my lost sheep. I love you my child.

Thank you my Lord.

April 7, 2005
My Lord, please share your wisdom with me this day.

I give you freely of my wisdom. You are called to handle it with care, to be my faithful steward of all I chose to share with you. It is sacred and you must be careful to release only when I make it very clear to you. My purpose will be fulfilled as you obey this very important lesson.

Yes, my Lord, I am counting on your Holy Spirit that you have put in me to give clear instruction.

My sheep know my voice. You will know what I Am speaking. It will be very clear, as I have told you. Be careful with time to release. Time is important. My plans are precise, and time is time when I say so. Be careful to put your flesh aside and you will be acting in my faith and confidence that will flow freely through your vessel of clay. When you see the clay, I see the gold. This is humility in my service. Yielded vessel of mine, I love you more than you can ever think or imagine. All is well. Meditate on my word and words. You are becoming an accomplished instrument for my purpose. I know what is best, trust in this.

Thank you my Lord.

April 11, 2005
My Lord, teach me how to help build your kingdom.

When you are weak, then I Am strong. Yield everything to me. I Am Creator of the universe, surely I can do all things I desire. Trust me as you have-continue to trust in me. All is well, all is on time.

Thank you my Lord for reminding me.

Come to me with all your cares and concerns. I will do what is best. Leave everything in my hands. I Am working with you to finish the work I have begun in you for my purpose. Look to me and hear me. Do not take all that man says as my words. Man is man-meek and frail-no matter how he strives toward me, he is merely man. I direct, I purify and I make holy my own vessels. Be wise and judge all things by my word and words I have spoken to you in my Spirit. My kingdom will come to this earth. It is on the way. Watch for it, be a wise watch-man on my wall. It is coming; it is on the way to completion. My Holy Spirit is working through my vessels of honor. Those who are totally

yielded to me, I will use. It is not of you, dear daughter, it is my working of my will, not yours. Be available to me. I Am looking and searching for yielded vessels. That is all I need, I do the purifying to make my vessels ready. Just yield- that is your job. Let me be the one to purify. I use any yielded vessel when I have the need. Be available and see me do the work. My Love, be at peace.

Thank you my Lord.

April 23, 2005
Praise and thank you my Lord. Do you have a special word for me today?

Come, take my hand and let us go to our higher place.

OK, my Lord, I'm ready to go. Use me for your Glory. Give me what I need to go.

You do not need anything to come with me. I have it all. Just hold my hand and let me guide and light

your pathway. We will meet and speak to many along the way. I'll give you proper words to say as I have promised. You can count on me to provide all you need. We will reap together, sweet daughter.

Yes, my Lord, this all sounds so beautiful but sometimes I think I imagine all this you have spoken to me.

Doubt not, trust and obey, I'll lead the way. You must trust me. You must rely on my strength and wisdom. I will provide everything you need to accomplish my purpose.

Thank you my Lord.

CHAPTER 6
Come With a Pure Heart.

Proverbs 20: 8&9
When a king sits on his throne to
judge, he winnows out all evil with
his eyes. Who can say, "I have kept
my heart pure; I am clean and
without sin?"

May 3, 2005
I need help. What do I do?

Today, yes today hear my voice.

I am trying to listen. What do you
have to tell me?

**I Am here in my throne room
where I Am always and forever. I
have not moved from my secret
place. I've been waiting with
patience for your visit. You are
important to me. Come early to me
in your weakness and I will make
you strong. I take pleasure in
strengthening you. I know all
things but you need to ask.**

OK, my Lord, I give you my tired
and weak body, show me again how

you can make me strong.

Did I not bring them to you as I have said, in your weakness? Did I not accomplish my purpose? You do not know the beginning from the end as I do, only I know the working of my own hand. All is well and all is being worked out. Watch and pray, sweet daughter, I'll be using you again soon.

Thank you my Lord.

May 9, 2005
I come to you again. What do I need to hear this day?

I love you forever and ever, from everlasting to everlasting. I will not hurt or harm you. You must depend on me and my words to help you. I have my plan and purpose for you. You are being used mightily for my purpose. When you are weak, then am I strong. Pray and praise me for my knowledge and wisdom. I know all and will use my knowledge and wisdom for my kingdom purposes. You need not be anxious but

trusting in me and what I know. I can and will work all for my good and purpose. All is for my pleasure. You are pleasing to me. Some will hear you when you speak my words. Those who are seeking will find me. Pray that they seek me in their dilemma. I give clear and true instruction. Pray that there hearts be softened. A hard heart and stiff neck are not looking for me.

Thank you, thank you tell me more.

Rest in me and what I have spoken to you. My word is my word. You can depend on it. My purpose will be accomplished, on earth as it is in heaven. Amen.

Thank you my Lord.

May 19, 2005
Give me direction this day my Lord.

Follow me and your path will be straight and perfect. I know where we should go. All is working for your good and my purpose. You can count on me.

Yes my Lord, I am trying to be faithful and true to you and your calling.

Hear me when I speak and do not fear to act. I Am with you. My faith will accomplish my purpose. Fear not to be my instrument I hold you and move you gently and with my purpose in mind. Do not fear to yield yourself to the Masters hands. His playing out is purposeful and perfect. Take my faith I give to you freely and abundantly for my purpose. Hear my voice when I speak. Fear me not. I will not harm or embarrass myself. As the potter molds and makes ready, I now use you my fine tuned instrument of honor. Let me hold you and play out my purpose and will through you. The melody will be sweet and true, pleasant to the ear that hears my voice. Sweet daughter, sweet child hear me and obey. I understand, fear not.

Thank you my Lord, here I am, send

me.

May 27, 2005
What is my lesson for today my
Lord?

**Lessons learned will be shared
lessons. Those who come to you,
who are seeking me will have the
ears to hear what the Spirit is
speaking and teaching. Lessons of
life, lessons of truth and wisdom
will flow from your lips. Do not be
afraid to speak truth and wisdom I
have shared with you to those I
Am sending to you. Be faithful to
me sweet daughter. I see all, I
know all and I can use all for my
purpose. Be careful to speak what
I give you in season. Time and
times are important. All works in
perfect order for my perfect plan.
I will go before you and behind
you to fulfill my perfect purpose.**

Thank you my Lord. I will listen to
your words and speak them in your
faith and confidence that you will
give to me freely.

My plan is loosing days. Time is so

short and the lost souls are many. Pray they are seeking wisdom and truth. As they seek, they will hear. I promise this in my word, so speak my words of wisdom in my faith and confidence, my beloved child.

Thank you my Lord.

June 2, 2005
My lord, do you have any advice for me today?

Take my hand, the one that has and holds all out to you. Take what you need my vessel of honor. I have told you many times that all you need has already been supplied. All you need to do is take what you need. I give it all to you freely. It is my gift to you sweet bride, sweet child. Just trust me and have faith in me. Look to me the one and only Almighty One. I know you and I understand your needs. They will be met. Ask and it shall be given to you freely.

Thank you my Lord. I do not want to be greedy. Help me to be grateful. I do give you permission to do as you wish with me.

June 3, 2005
My Lord, am I fit for the battle?

You are fit for the battle. Keep on the full armor. Let me keep you dressed. My cover will be around and about you. I Am your cover and protection as I send you forth to do battle in my name and for my kingdom. A new thing is being established. My kingdom has come. Add to my kingdom soldiers fit for my purpose. The battle has already been won. Understanding will come to you as you need it. Just come with me into the battlefields. The harvest is in the fields. You need only to come and stand your position. I will place you in the correct position. I will go before you, I will be with you. I will give you great words of wisdom, all has been established. Be there with me, my instrument of honor and grace. Great is your calling. Recognize this. Be not afraid of where you will be sent. Now is the accepted time of the

**Lord. Master of all, King of Kings
is my beloved Son. You too are my
beloved child of my Child.
Understand your position. Take it
up and go forward. The battle
sound has been piped. You are
called to a higher position. Do
battle in my name. The war has
been won. Confidence in me and
my direction. Up, I say up higher
is the call. Focus on me. Do not fall
to the lies of the enemy. Look up I
say, look up to me. I Am high and
above all that is or ever will be.
Come with me sweet child of
grace.**

Thank you my Lord. Take me up and
hold me there.

June 15, 2005
Give me encouragement to go
forward I do not want to be stuck in
a neutral place.

**Pure and true is my cover of
righteousness over you. Be not
troubled, but confident in my
cover. You are protected from all
evil. Do not let that evil one disturb
your peace. Your prayers have**

been heard. I Am taking care of everything. So, relax and praise my name.

Yes my Lord, I do know this, but I allow my flesh to suffer pain. Help me let go of this unnecessary worry. I know it does not please you. I also know it pleases you to be my help in time of need.

All will come together, just keep your focus on me and my word and words. I will take care of everything. All is well.

Thank you my Lord.

June 27, 2005
As I come to you in the righteousness of Jesus, what will you have me do.

Praise me, praise me the Mighty One, the all in all the one who sits above all that is and ever will be. My hand, my mighty hand is extended to you. All that is rests in my hand, a hand outstretched to you, with all that you need. See me and see my hand outstretched ever

so eager to give to you all you can ask or think. Would a Father deny his child when he comes in faith believing that all the Father has he freely shares with his children, I think not. Be encouraged in me. Look to me and you will find me. I Am high and lifted up. Come up and sit with me, high above all that is and see what I see. I will reveal and I will share my wisdom with you. So rest and come to me. Do not strive just come. Seek and come.

Thank you my Lord.

July 1, 2005
Do you have a word for me today?

All is well. Your soul magnifies the Lord. Do not pay attention to your flesh. Your Spirit is in good control. I Am here to help in time of your need. You do not always recognize my hand. But I Am doing for you things you cannot see. I love you, that is why I take such good care of you and your needs.

But Lord, what can I do for you. I wait and I see little.

You are doing when you do not realize it. Just live your life and let my light shine through. You may not see what you do for me but others see and make a note of it.

July 21, 2005
What do I need this day?

Comfort. Let me be your comforter. Let me wrap you in my blanket of love. From everlasting to everlasting. I love you with unconditional love. Let me be your all in all. I will never ever leave or forsake you. Know this. I Am true to my word. You need not know all I Am doing but you can know for sure that my love is everlasting, true and unconditional.

Thank you my Lord. I know this in my spirit, but my flesh is weak. Help me to look to my spirit.

Look and see that I Am good. I Am just and all will come to pass for your good and my purpose. My

ways are far above all you can ask or think. Be my trusting child. Be confident in me as your Father. I know all your needs and I know all your cares. Just cast your cares to me in confidence that I have already done all that needs doing for the good of all concerned. Some good will seem harsh to your flesh-just trust in my judgment. It is just and it is true. Read my word and understand my judgments. All is well and all is in perfect harmony to my time. I love you my sweet child. Fret not.

Thank you my father.

July 23, 2005
Here am I Lord. Where will you send me?

Your praises are sent to the uttermost parts of the universe. I can hear you. Can you hear me and my instruction? Praise me, praise me for I have all in control.

July 28, 2005
Praise you my Lord.

**Thank you for your praises, my
sweet daughter. Now you are
beginning to understand me and
my ways. All has been established
before the foundation of the earth
and all will be accomplished. As
you rest in my finished work and
sing my praises, I can now bring
all things together for my purpose.
All was established long ago and
all will come to pass.**

August 5, 2005
Good morning, my Lord. I praise
you this day and wait for
instructions.

**Good plan my sweet child my
sweet daughter. You are becoming
wise in your understanding of me.
Keep vigilant and alert. You will
hear my voice and know what to
say and do. All is well.**

Thank you my Lord. Help my faith
to do what you instruct me to do.

**You will know what to do and say
and I will provide my faith for you
to accomplish my goal. Be not
afraid to speak what I give you at**

the time I give you to speak. It will be my perfect time to accomplish my purpose. Do not be concerned at what you think you see with your eyes. Be only concerned with what you hear in you spirit. Spirit speaks to spirit. Your spirit in my faith speaks to man in the uttermost parts of the world. My will, will be done. Being vigilant and alert speeds up the process. I Am depending on my children to hear and do as I instruct.

Praise you my Lord.

August 10, 2005
My Lord, what do I need to know?

Wisdom!

What about wisdom my Lord.

Guard it. My wisdom that I share with you should be guarded with great care. Not to do so is tragic. Wisdom should be wisely spent. I will show you clearly when to invest it. My investments always yield a high profit when spent at the proper time. Praise me and

hold wisdom until I release the power to spend it.

Thank you my Lord. Help me to be alert. Reveal your presence when it is time to spend.

Not to worry. Be confident in Me and My knowledge. Knowledge released at the proper time is wisdom. I'll show you clear passage. Don't abort the ship.

Thank you my Lord.

CHAPTER 7
Put No Other gods Before Me.

Deuteronomy 3:24
"O Sovereign Lord, you have begun to show to your servant your greatness and your strong hand. For what god is there in heaven or on Earth who can do the deeds and mighty works you do."

August 19, 2005
Thank you for all that you do for me. Praise your Holy Name. Teach me more about your name.

My name is above all that is.
My name is pure Majesty.
My name is the solid Rock.
My name is Holy, Holy, Holy.
My name is creations Source.
My name is worthy of all praise on earth and heaven above.
Amen.

August 30, 2005
My Lord, do you have a special task for us this day. Thank you for using us.

Darkness comes quickly now. Be alert and hear what I Am telling you. You are my light that will shine in the darkness. Those who see you will recognize you are different. Answer what they ask you. Be wise and do not overwhelm them. You must be all things to all people as my church comes from all corners of the earth. Some will heed your advice and turn to me. Some will not come. Pray they have ears to hear and eyes to see what I Am doing. Be faithful and true to me. Do not strive or struggle as my way is love and peace. Understand I Am gentle and merciful and you must be also. Darkness cannot stay in the light. That is why some you love and pray for will flee from your very presence. They will avoid you because they love the darkness. Let them go and continue to pray for them. Maybe later they will look for the light. My ways are easy and my burden is light.

September 5, 2005

What?

Father, I Am your Father. I sit high and lifted up above all that is. You can find me also in the low places. I Am, with you in all of life's trials and tribulations. Know that I Am always with you, in you, around you, everywhere you are I Am. I will never leave or abandon you. You know I Am true to my word.

Thank you my Father for this. What special thing do I need to know for this day?

As I Am true to you, be true to me. We can do great and wondrous things when we stick together in the knowledge of each other. We will move mountains together in the strength and wisdom of God Almighty. Keep a sharp ear for my direction as you go through this glorious day I have made for you. Be glad in it and for it. Sit with me and see what I see this day. With no thought of tomorrow, be confident I will also take care of tomorrow. All is established; all

**will turn out precisely as I have
planned before the foundation of
the earth. I Am, I Am, and I Am.
Amen.**

Thank you my Lord.

September 10, 2005
Glory to your name my Father. What
do you have for me today?

Wealth.

What kind of wealth my Lord and
thank you for it?

**Your need is for divine wealth.
The wealth I share with you is only
given to a few. You will receive
what you ask for and much more**

Awesome, my Lord. It is hard for me
to comprehend.

**All that I possess can be your tool
when I place it in your hand. Do
not be greedy, but wise. Spend it
with great care and discernment.
Do not allow your flesh to
interfere. Let my Spirit in you
dominate. You can take dominion**

over what I have given to man. It belongs to you. I do not need it. I gave it to you. Do not allow what is already yours to sit in waste. As you take and use what is already yours, it will shine and be holy. Properly used it is holy. Improperly used it is waste.

Thank you my Lord. I am depending on your guidance to use what I have in holiness and wisdom.

That is good, my sweet child. Do not struggle or fret. I'll take care of all. You are my gifted vessel. Relax and stay alert.

September 21, 2005
How can I receive my inheritance in you? I know it is there, how does it manifest itself now?

Timing is everything. As soon as the pieces are in their designated positions, the puzzle will be complete. Life is a puzzle and the pieces are placed perfectly and with great care. All things have a purpose, yet they are just things. Eternal rewards are forever and

ever. Seek what is eternal. Do not seek the temporal.

Help me to understand in a deeper way. My Lord.

My glory is yours. Let me pour it out of you onto others. The more I pour the more there is. Endless glory. As you let me give it away it increases again and again. Let the supernatural be natural for you. A way of life with great purpose and conviction. Many will come into my kingdom and many will not. Free will dominates. Each one must learn to give it over to me and my purpose. Be wise in my Spirit. Gentle and loving with great care. Gentle love wins the body to me. Fret not about your own needs, my supply is at hand. Plant and sow, plant and sow. Give out what you expect to receive. You plant and sow. Harvest is in due season. Everything in its proper place and proper time. Your part is to plant and sow. I Am the King of the Harvest.

Praise your holy and perfect plan.

September 29, 2005
What is it I need to know for today?

Darkness, great darkness will soon cover the earth. Be prepared to stand for me. It is not going to be an easy journey, but you can know I Am with you always. Even to the end of time. Time as you know it now. Be willing to simply rest in me. You will need to keep a sharp ear, as great confusion will surround you. Know also that I Am not the author of confusion. Be aware of where it comes from. I have overcome the evil one, the battle HAS BEEN WON. Rest in this in the midst of confusion. All will come to completion as I have planned from the foundation of the earth. Go forward in confidence that this is my will. Great light will come forth out of great darkness. Light always wins. Fear not, have faith in me. I will supply all.

Thank you for telling me these things. Help me to be faithful to you only. Help your bride overcome this confusion. Help us to focus on you,

the Creator and sustainer of all that
is.

**Share now what I Am revealing to
you, some will hear and some will
run from you. Pray for those that
are lost and will not acknowledge
the light. You are a chosen vessel
for my light. Let it shine, let it
shine, let it shine.**

Thank you Jesus.

September 30, 2005
My Lord, what is your priority for
today?

**My priority is for me to know.
Your priority is to praise and trust
in me. Relax; know I Am with you
and I Am for you. Your best
interests are the priority of my
heart. Beat, Beat. You make my
heart beat. My love for you
overwhelms my heart. Passion for
you overwhelms my heart. We are
bonded together at the heart. Two
hearts beating together as one.
Come to that place in me where
you move in my heart to fulfill my
desires. Move with me and not**

apart from me and see if I do not show you great and mighty things accomplished in my name and in my power. Move gently with great purpose. My purpose, to win the hearts of many to my bosom, so I may hold them close to my heart as I hold you. Share my joy. Move with me as we together win the hearts of the lost. Each one a special jewel in my crown. Sweet daughter, yield to me and see if our hearts are not but one. I love you.

Thank you my awesome friend and lover of my heart.

October 14, 2005
(Mother's 85th birthday)
I'm trying to spend the day with you my Lord. What do I need to know?

I Am your Father and your Mother.

Pretty strange Lord. You never told me you were my Mother. What does this mean?

I Am all in all. Everything you

need. Your nourishment and nurturing comes from me. I Am there for you always until the end of time of which there is no end. Whatever your need, you can depend on me with all my love and all your need. I Am not flesh and blood that can hurt or disappoint you. I Am Spirit and Truth and I Am true to my word. Study my word and believe what I teach you. Truth through my Spirit equals unconditional love.

Thank you my Lord. Teach me all I need to know to be all I need to be.

You are exactly where you should be today do not try to understand my ways. You will know just what you need to know. Remember to let the supernatural be natural in you and through you. Let my Holy Spirit flow freely through you. Relax in my faith I give to you to let it flow. Rest in this my sweet daughter. My loved of the Beloved. Bonded together in my love.

Thank you. Thank you. Thank you.

October 17, 2005
My Lord, teach me more of this
Father-Mother relationship I have
with you.

**Come, let me hold you and teach
you more. We are family and all I
have is yours. As all you have
should be mine. We are not like
human family that can withhold
and hurt. We are whole and holy
together bonded in a covenant of
pure love. Remember, all you have
is mine and all I have is yours. As
you give it up to me, I can release
and give it over to you. Now rest in
this. Be ready to release when I say
give.**

You make it sound so easy. You
need to help me bury the flesh and
seek you in the Spirit.

**You are doing fine. Growth takes
time. It cannot be rushed. The
fullness takes a lifetime. Fullness of
what is possible. Some never see or
entertain my Glory. It is there. We
will call it forth. It lives in the
grave of dead flesh. It must come
forth as Lazareth came forth anew**

**from dead flesh in my Spirit, so too
you can come forth in my Glory
from death of your flesh.
Abundant Glory can be released.
Work with me as you rest. All is
well. I love you sweet daughter.**

Thank you my Lord.

October 20, 2005
I'm tired in my body. I don't know
why. Help me.

Energize!

How?

**Keep plugged into me. I have all
the answers. They will come just
when you need them. Soak up
now. Relax and renew your spirit
in me.**

I'll try my best. Thank you my Lord.

October 26, 2005
What? I know you have something
big to tell me.

**Come sweet child, come up to my
lap. Let me hold you. When a child**

**sits on Dad's lap, she can ask
whatever she wants. If it is in
Dad's power to give to his child
and if it is for the child's good, she
will have what she asks for. So,
what do you want sweet child?**

I want all that you have for me. All
that was pre-destined for your
purpose and for your Glory.

**That is the correct answer. I Am
ready now to pour and pour into
you my power and my glory for
the good of the brethren. Give out,
give out and it will return to you
many fold. My glory will increase
and grow as you unselfishly give it
away. My glory is passing through
your vessel of honor. Don't waste
my time holding onto it. It is to
share with the brethren.**

Awesome, my Lord. Please confirm
this. I do not want to be out of order.

November 2, 2005
Teach me more by your Holy Spirit.

**Come, let us worship together.
Give and take. All that is mine is**

**yours and visa-versa. Tap into my
power. Let it flow. I Am with you
now and for ever to direct the flow.
Let it go. Now is the accepted time
of the Lord. Lord of all, King of
Kings, from everlasting to
everlasting. Down from the wall is
your NOW position. You have
seen the world and now minister to
their needs. Release what you
know and let my Holy Spirit do the
rest.**

Yes, I will my Lord. I'll need your
help as I take my step of faith in your
faith.

**This is good. We need to work this
through together. You take what I
have and I'll use what you have.
Together we will accomplish great
and mighty things for the
Kingdom of God. My Kingdom
has come. Spread the word to the
brethren.**

I'll do my best. I know you will be
faithful. I'll need lots of your help to
do my part.

November 10, 2005
What time is it my Lord?

**See the sea of humanity. They are
drowning and being overcome in
the great floods of there sin. Time
will be spent to wash them clean.
When no place is left for them to
put there foot, they will then see
me. They will come to me and my
kingdom. Time of great darkness
and then comes the light. Pray and
praise are due me as my plan is
just and true. They will come, but
most will not. Pray and praise and
stay alert. Time moves fast now
and judgment will be swift. Be not
perplexed as the sun shines on the
just and unjust so too darkness
will fall on the just and unjust.
Hold fast as you see all these things
that must come to pass as I save a
few through this.**

Keep me alert and if it be thy will,
give me power to make a difference.

**You have the power as I have told
you. Step out and use what we
have together. Remember, what is**

mine is yours and what is yours is mine. I can use all you have and visa versa. Trust in what I Am telling you again, all is there. Give me all you have as I have given you all I have. A two-edged sword working together for the good of all the brethren. I'm trusting you to use all wisely. Believe in me as I believe in my Father.

Thank you my Lord.

CHAPTER 8
Focus On Me, the One True God.

John 17: 1-5
After Jesus said this, he looked
toward heaven and prayed: "Father,
the time has come. Glorify your Son,
that your Son may glorify you. For
you granted him authority over all
people that he might give eternal life
to all those you have given him. Now
this is eternal life: that they may
know you, the only true God, and
Jesus Christ, whom you have sent. I
have brought you glory on earth by
completing the work you gave me to
do. And now, Father, glorify me in
your presence with the glory I had
with you before the world began."

November 16, 2005
What?

We are standing in the throne
room at the feet of Lord God
Almighty. He is pleased that we
have come. He has set this time
aside just for us.

I bow down to your majesty, of all
you are that I do not understand.

What would you like from me?

All you are and all you have is mine. How wonderful to see you. Listen and hear and you will see me. Lend me your ear and I will fill it from on high. You have been elevated to a higher place-to a higher call. Be humbled as I have chosen you-you have not chosen me.

I sincerely thank you. You know how weak I am and that I'm just learning to listen.

Not to worry. I Am teaching you. You will go forward and not backward. We will go together in my Holy Spirit to places both familiar and strange. I Am with you in front, behind, inside and all around. Just go with the flow. Beautiful daughter, beautiful one I Am well pleased with you. Be ready in season and out of season. Do not concern yourself with details, just step out now. Trust me to provide all you need to complete the task. Do not concern yourself with results. You will accomplish

**all I have set before you. Be brave
and true to my call. I do not call
everyone, but I have called and
chosen you. You have passed the
test and the promotion has been
granted. Rejoice in me as I Am
rejoicing in you, sweet daughter,
sweet child.**

Praise God. Thank you for the
promotion. I'll try my best to make
you proud.

November 21, 2005
Thank you for all you do for me.
How can I bless you back?

**Holy Glory. Our union generates
Holy Glory. Step out as I have
shown you. Yes, I will meet you as
you step forward. I too am with
you to go forward in glorious
divine faith. The kind of faith that
moves mountains. We will make a
way where there is no way. I Am
God and I can do this. I need your
body to work with me. As Jesus
worked through a body, I now am
working by my Holy Spirit
through your body. Time is here to
accomplish great things for my**

kingdom. We are in a different place. A place of power and might. The power and glory of my Spirit revealed to mankind. Even seeing, some will not believe.

How can I help? I give you my body to use. It is not perfect, but I know you can use it.

Thank you. I'll take it. Some think they have given me all, but have not. I can take what appears to be imperfect and make it perfect in every way for I Am God. I Am just waiting patiently for my children to release to me all they have. I in turn will release all I have. Now is the accepted hour. The world is waiting for it knows not what. I will soften their hearts. I will open their eyes. I will do all I can to make them hear. But still many reject me and hold fast to the world. I weep for them as they make their choices.

Thank you my Lord.

November 25, 2005
Why did I have such a bad week?

What am I supposed to be learning from this?

Keep your mouth shut and your eyes open. I will show you what it is you are to learn.

Please tell me now.

You are a chosen vessel unto me. I will cleans and polish as I see fit. The more the pressure, the stronger the gold. All my love you will behold. When you feel weak, I then will make you strong. Lessons learned are lessons shared. Closed lips through the fire will bring great rewards. When it is over, be ready to share. Time will present itself to share what you have learned. I Am making you ready to speak in my anointed power of my word. Give out and it will be given back, my word, my lessons learned. Pure gold made stronger for my purpose.

Thank you my Lord.

December 2, 2005
What are you telling your body

today, my Lord?

**Listen to me, hear what I say. I
Am sitting in my throne room. I
Am ready to teach you. Listen.**

OK, I'm listening. What is it my
Lord?

**You are insignificant, yet you are
all I need. Insignificant in that you
can do nothing for my kingdom on
your own. You are all I need, in
that I need all of your body. I have
told you again and again, just to
rest in me and give all you have.
Your imperfect self has been
remolded into my golden vessel of
honor. I will have my way as you
have yielded all to me for my
purpose. Rest, hear and obey. Do
not struggle on your own as it will
come to not. Rest and flow with me
and we will accomplish all I have
planned and purposed. To do
otherwise, only slows down the
process. Time is running out fast
now and there is a lot left to do.
The pressure is on my chosen
vessels to hear me and obey. Do
not get caught up in your good**

**works, but yield to my good
working through you.**

Why does my flesh sometimes hear
double talk when you speak?

**Because your flesh can be double
minded, but my Spirit in you has a
single eye and it is set on things
that are far above human
thinking. Thanks for asking. I like
this. It gives me a chance to
explain heavenly things. All is well
and I Am proud of you as you are
doing the best you know to do. Do
not be fearful, but confident in my
Holy Spirit to complete all that is
set before you. One step at a time
you are growing up just fine.
Continue to be mine with all you
have and all you are. It is higher,
deeper and wider than you can
ever imagine. Mighty works are
being done through you. I can see
what you cannot see yet. You are
blessed as you bless me. I weep
tears of joy over you. Be humble.
Be still. I Am here.**

Thank you my Lord.

December 6, 2005
What?

**Come unto me all you who labor
and are heavy-burdened and I will
give you rest.**

Show me the way my Lord.

**Rest and be renewed in my Spirit.
Let me do this for you. You are
struggling and striving. I have told
you not to do that. I will give you
the rest you need. I will comfort
and sustain you. Let go and let me
do this.**

OK, my lord, my desire is to obey
this. Meet me where I am and carry
me through. You know my
weakness.

**I Am lifting you, relax and focus
on me and I will help you.**

Thanks my Lord.

December 11, 2005
Praises and thanks to my Lord.
Teach me something new.

When you are weary then am I the strongest? When you are void of yourself, I can be strongest in myself through you. You are learning well. Do not procrastinate or hesitate when my Spirit is ready to move through you. You will know it is me, there will be no doubt.

How will you be using me, my Lord?

You are my pot. My pot to fill and my pot to empty. Be still-be humble-be ready-just BE. You have no needs for yourself. For you will know that all has already been provided. You are learning to trust me to provide as my will sees fit. You have all you need for today. All you need for tomorrow has also been provided. Portion comes one day at a time. Rest in confidence in my provision for you. I Am provider, I Am source, I Am all in all. I will not disappoint you. Come and yield to me.

OK

December 15, 2005

I do not know my own needs.
Thanks for knowing and providing.

**I Am your very present help in
your time of need. I Am ready,
willing and able to help you way
beyond your needs of the moment.
You are mine and have been since
before the foundation of the earth.
I Am taking great care and pride
in you. You are among my chosen
vessels. You are more ready and
able than you realize. I will use my
chosen vessels for my purpose. I
have a master plan that you
cannot understand all of right
now. But you are a precious part
of my plan as my chosen. Keep my
vessel clean and ready at all times
as you do not know exactly what
or when you are being used. Honor
me with all yourself as you live day
by day. You are mine-I Am yours.
Together we are doing mighty
things for my kingdom.**

What a privilege and honor. I'll do
my best to please you.

**I know you will. This is one reason
I have chosen you. You have not**

chosen me. Many are the called, but few are the chosen. My vessel of sweet honor and grace. You cannot know now how much I love you. It is overwhelming. All my love I share with you. I Am love and all I have I give to you. All! Think on this.

Thank you my Lord.

December 27, 2005
My spirit is trusting you but my flesh is weary. Help me to honor you in spite of myself.

Cover me? No! Do not cover me with yourself. Uncover and reveal me through yourself and your selflessness. You know who I Am. Realize I Am even when you are caught up and dragged down by yourself. Push through. Be persistent. Let me out to do my will and what I do. Do not of yourself. Break open the alabaster box. Let my sweet smell out. What I do is sweet and pleasant. Open the box and let me out. Do not be uptight; be relaxed and confident of what I have put into you. I have

spent my self on you. Let my Spirit flow forth as I have planned. Focus on Me and My finished work. When you are tight and tense in your flesh, you are holding me back. Let me out, let me flow and sweeten the air. My sweet smelling will savor a dead situation. I Am life, and life will flow from death. As I have told you before, death to self. Do not give place to self. Give me place and space to fill with my love and grace. I Am full of mercy and grace but you must give me a place to deposit and move from. I need you to make me a place. Do not deny me. Open the box, do not leave it closed tightly. Open, open and let me flow forth. My love, my sweet vessel of honor, let me teach you. Obey my words. Do not give my place to the wrong spirit. I Am the Spirit of love and truth. Hear ye me.

Thank you my Lord.

December 29, 2005
Cover me my Lord. I give you permission to cover me and my own will.

You are uncovered and exposed to the elements. Battles will come but Oh! sweet victory is yours. Do not focus on the battle as I have already won it for you. Focus on me and sweet victory will be yours. It has been paid in full. Take advantage of the truth. I Am the author and finisher of all truth. Do not waste too much time in the battle. Victory! Forward march.

I am trying to understand. You need to help me and carry me through the battle.

I have been with you through each one and I will never, never leave you alone. When you feel you are alone, try to remember that you are not alone. I Am with you always, my chosen vessel of great honor. One day, one portion of provision at a time. Do not get out of step. I Am leading you into the paths you must follow to accomplish my perfect will for you in my kingdom. All is well with your soul sweet child.

I love you my Lord for reassuring me now.

January 2, 2006
We need each other. What is my part for today?

Stand. Your job is to stand firm in my truth. Do not hesitate today to speak my truth in love when the opportunity presents itself. Truth and justice will prevail. Good will overcomes evil every time. My daughter, we are of the same bloodline.

Thank you my Lord.
January 12, 2006
What do you need me to know today?

Today is all you have. Yesterday is gone and tomorrow has been taken care of. Make the most of all there is for today. All I have is for you and at your disposal. Spend it well. Do not waste my precious gifts to you. Share them with those who will be sent to you today. Do not struggle or strive, let it come from you gently and naturally. Set

yourself to one side and let me flow with my love, truth and knowledge from you, my sweet vessel of honor. I Am taking you at your word that you are at my disposal. Know I Am always at your disposal with all I have to share with those that come to you. I have led them by my Spirit as I can see the longing of the hearts of those who know not what they are seeking. Be assured that all is perfect and precise. All is exactly on time. Remember that my time is different from your time. It is important to pray and let them come to you. All is well, my sweet child. Rest and know me. My love.

Thank you my Lord.

January 20, 2006
Here I am Lord.

Quiet, be still and know that I Am your God. Ever present, forever your present help in time of need. You have nothing to fear. I Am all you need. Have faith in this. Everything is working out for your good and my purpose. You are in

**the palm of my hand as you seek to
know me. You seek my face and I
hold you in my hand along with all
you need.**

Thank you.

January 26, 2006
My Lord, teach me something I do
not know re-seeing into the spiritual
realm. I'm confused.

**Confusion does not come from me.
I Am all knowledge and wisdom.
Set your eyes on me, the Author
and Finisher of all things.**

Lord, I know you are not the master
of confusion. What should I do? I
know there are things I do not see.
Should I seek to see into this
dimension?

**Time and space, give my kingdom
time and space. As I have told you
before, time is my way of weighing
and balancing all that is for my
purpose. As you have made a place
for me you also make a space for
me to bring you into another place.**

**You cannot struggle with my
work, as the supernatural will
happen very naturally when TIME
and SPACE come together. Relax
in my confidence to bring them
together. Again, it is not anything
you should be striving for. It is
simple faith in what I can and will
do. Just spend time with me and
let me be God. You cannot control
me but you can invite me and rest
in results. It's a different place
that can only be reached by
trusting and resting in me. I know
what is best. Relax!**

Thanks for explaining.

February 1, 2006
STOP and WRITE

**Come to me. You have left your
first love. Seek me and rest in my
promises. You need not struggle
and strive. When you do, you bind
my Spirit and give permission to
the evil one, learn this lesson and
come to me in confidence of what
has already been established from
the beginning of time. Do not bind
my Holy Spirit in you. Rest in my**

work that has been established from before the foundation of the universe. Do not let your free will lean to your flesh. Seek my face and I will direct you. My path is straight and sure. See this simple lesson and let go of your flesh and walk in my Holy Spirit. My love, my love I wait and weep. Seek to see and know me for who I Am. I Am faithful, I will reveal myself to you. Rest, let go of self and hold onto me. I will not let you go. When storms arise, I Am holding you to my very bosom. I will not allow you to be swept away. You are mine and I Am yours. Be still my sweet daughter and rest in me. The one who was, is, and forever shall be. Can you see that all is done and complete? Come to me.

Thank you my Lord. Keep me close and use this vessel for your purpose.

February 3, 2006
Father God, please teach me something new today.

Confidence in me and what has been done. You are in that place of

rest, confidence and faith. You are yielded to my will and I will use you as I choose. My chosen one.

Yes my Lord, I feel I do know all this. Please teach me something I do not yet realize.

As the sun rises early in the morning, so too I rise up and reach out to those who will seek me early in each day.

Why is this my Lord?

To teach you that it is in rest that I come and do my best work. All is complete as I pull together all the necessary pieces to accomplish my will for the day. So seek me early and you will find me.

Thank you my Lord.

February 27, 2006
What orders do you have for me today my Lord?

I Am taking you up higher to my secret place today. That special place reserved for my elected and

chosen. You will know me in a deeper way. Again a paradox. I take you higher so you may know me deeper. There are so many facets of myself I would like to reveal to you. We go together with ease and gently. This road we travel together is a slow journey. You must go slowly so as to observe what is all around you. As we travel together down an unknown path, you must look around and observe the beauty. All of creation, all the landscape, all of what is above, below, in front and behind. All of what I do around you as we go. You may not recognize all I am doing, but others are watching. When you feel stuck or in neutral, others are watching you. They are being touched by your life as we travel along together. When you think you are standing still, I Am working it all out. Know this, I love you and all is part of my plan.

Thank you my Lord. Give me eyes to see what you are doing. Give me vision for your purpose. I wish to honor you with my life.

February 28, 2006
What is your wisdom for me today
my Lord?

**Come closer. Take my hand. Let
me help you walk before me at my
throne. Climb up on my lap and
let me protect you. Santa Clause!
Let me be your Santa Clause,
sweet child and tell me what you
want. I know what I have for you,
but you must ask in faith believing.
You will be surprised, as what you
will receive is much greater than
what you will ask for. Trust in me
and my choices. I know the value
of things better than you. I will not
give you a rock when you are only
asking for bread. It is written, I
am your Father. Climb down now
from my lap and go in peace this
day. Your Father has his hand on
you and with his tender love and
care He is guiding you along your
pathway of life everlasting.**

Thank you my Father.

March 11, 2006
What's new for today my Lord?

Peacock, strut and hold your head high.

What are you trying to tell me my Lord?

You have done nothing wrong in my sight. So you can hold your head high and walk before me.

What about peacock?

Brilliant multi-colors. Like the colors of my rainbow.

I still do not understand peacock.

You are my beautiful creation for me to enjoy. I see your beauty when you see none. For my own pleasure I have created and designed you.

March 16, 2006
Good morning my Lord. Do I have a special assignment today?

Stand firm in all I have taught you.

Okay my Lord, I'll do my best.

I know you will. I'll be with you to help and guide you. Do not be afraid of the words that come from your mouth. They are power and truth to the lost and a guide to those who believe in me. We will encourage both together. It is our joint assignment. To seek and save those who are lost. They hunger for truth. Feed my sheep. You are my blessed vessel of honor. Release what I have put in you and more will come into you. You cannot out give me sweet daughter, sweet friend, I love you.

Thank you my Lord.

March 17, 2006
Thanks for a beautiful day. Open my ears and speak to me.

Be still my child and hear my creation. They sing to me, sweet music to my ears. I get such pleasure from all my created beings. Each one different and unique. It should be no great surprise to you that I get great

pleasure from you. All you say and do is for my pleasure. I understand you and where you are coming from. I also understand where you are going. So just come along with me as I guide you into greater truths of my kingdom. We travel together, you and I. Do not be too surprised at all I am going to share with you, my faithful one. I see you and the true desires of your heart.

Soon now! What my Lord?

Soon now I will release into your care great responsibilities. Do not fear. I Am with you every step of the way. We will step out together into deeper waters. Refreshed and ready to go.

Where will we go my Lord?

We will go to the streets and the byways. To people great and small. Open your mouth and speak what I have given you. Freely you have received, so freely give out and share what you have. I Am by your side to uphold and guide you. In my Spirit you will accomplish

much. All that I have set before you will prosper. My word will not return to me void. It is written and it will come to pass. Go in confidence with my blessing. My sweet one, my faithful one. I love you.

Thank you my Lord, I am ready. Move through me by your Spirit as you have said, I release you as you have released me.

March 19, 2006
What are we going to do today my Lord?

Come to my table and eat what I have prepared for you. All is good even the bitter herbs. Bitter is bad to the taste but good for the body. Cleansing and purging of my body is taking place. You cannot see all now but I will reveal my truths to you. Trust in me and follow after my Spirit. I will not lead you down the wrong path. But you must keep your eye on Me and follow where I Am leading YOU. Hold me tightly, I will never let you go as you are looking at and to Me.

Thank you my Lord. Please help me to see you and know your mind.

My mind has one purpose and I will bring it to pass. I Am, God and I can do this.

Yes My Lord.

March 20, 2006

Opportunities will come your way to speak of Me and glorify My name. The name that is above all that is. Do not fear but trust in my word. You will have increased wisdom on how to deal with people. You will be all things to all people. You will win their hearts by compassion and wisdom.

Yes my Lord, I am counting on your help. My body is really tired, but I know you will strengthen me for the task.

March 22, 2006
What will we do together in the future? This vessel is ready for the assignments you have for me.

OK, Let's go. One step at a time, one day at a time. Where you go, I go. We are bonded together in love. Love and compassion will be shared with those we meet along the way. Be gentle in my Spirit and speak what I have taught you. Release and walk away as my Spirit in them will be ignited to work in them.

I desire to know more about what we will do.

True peace on earth. Heaven will be released through you. All the planning through the generations will come together on earth. It will melt and fold together. It will create a new earth for my chosen. Eternity will be spent on earth but we must get it ready. What is true will remain, what is of the old system or worldly system, will be done away with. The finished will finally be finished. Peace on earth, good will to men. When only my Spirit remains, there will be true peace on earth.

What will my physical body be like as we together approach the lost sheep?

Wholly mine.

Yes, I'll be wholly yours, but will I be wholly healed body, soul and spirit?

Yes you will. Will it, grasp it and release it by the power I have given over to you. All I have belongs to you for your purpose. Purpose to be healed body, soul and spirit. It has been paid for and it has been ordered. Pick up your order. I give it over to you.

OK, I will to take total healing body, soul and spirit.

March 27, 2006
Share more of your knowledge with me my Lord.

Take wisdom and share it along with my knowledge. One is not good without the other. Open your ears and hear what I speak and

teach you.

I am here Lord, to hear what you have for me.

Grace and mercy will follow you all the days of your life. You will be my guide to the blind. Hope for the hopeless. Healing to the sick at heart. My faith in you will heal the sick in body. My Spirit in you will heal the sick in spirit. Open your mouth and speak what I have taught you in wisdom and knowledge. My lessons are from the Master of all there is. I know all, see all, hear all and I'll share with you to help the lost to see Me. What I speak to you is sure and true. You can depend on Me all the time. Be not anxious as I alert you to the lost and seeking. They will know it is Me in you. Gently, gently is the way to woo my children.

I'm counting on you and your Holy Spirit in me to make wise choices and speak wise words.

My love, my sweet daughter, my

**sweet friend, go now. You have all
you need to accomplish what I
have set before you. All, I say all I
have is at you disposal. You will
use it with great wisdom and
knowledge. It is great
responsibility that you will handle
well. Not to fear. Be bold in love.**

Help me my Lord to do my best.

April 10, 2006
Take me deeper into your being.
Teach me more about yourself.

**This is a tall order but I can
handle it. I've been waiting to
share more of myself with you
sweet daughter. All, I say all I have
and am, are at your disposal.
Through my Holy Spirit we will
accomplish great and mighty
things.**

How do I tap into this power that is
only in you.

**Easy, just step into me. You are
not ignorant of my power and
presence. It (power) will come
when you need it. In the meantime,**

praise me and rest. Hear me, as I have told you in the past. It is all right at hand. You will know me and my power when you need it. Not all will be healed, not all will experience my best because all will not believe and seek me out in that way. You, my child, are a chosen vessel to contain and release as you see fit. You will be sensitive to my release of power through your vessel of honor. Just be, and be alert to my Holy Spirit in you. A way will be made where you have not seen a way before. All is coming together in this time of great harvest. Greater than has ever been on the face of the earth since I created it. All will be new each day. The same old, same old is just to old. A new thing, a new thing, a new thing. Rejoice and praise my Holy name. You will see a move in my new thing. Do not look to the right or to the left. Only look strait ahead as we move forward together to meet the quota set before us. It is harvest time. Sing a new song of praise to me. You will hear the birds of the air singing to me this new song. They know me and sing to me this new song. They know no interference as they are my Holy creation. Doing what birds do and singing they're songs of pure and holy praise. They see no interruption in my plans, it is only man that has taken so long to know me. I have waited and wept and now it is time to dry my own tears and release what man is now ready to receive in this new way. Come up to me and ride above all the confusion and see how simple it is to connect with me and watch the harvest come in. Tools are prepared to gather in the crop. We will move quickly now in my Spirit through the golden vessels of honor. Do not fear, but praise my holy name. I have all things under control. Be blessed in knowing me and my purpose.

Praise you my Lord for sharing more of yourself with me.

April 20, 2006
My Lord, thank you for choosing me. Where will you send me and what will I do for your kingdom?

Red, I see red.

What does this mean?

You are covered by the righteous blood of Jesus. You are hidden in Him. You can go where you please. There are a lot of lost people out there. Your presence will separate the sheep from the goats, as the righteous blood that covers you will convict them. They themselves will choose the right or the left. Do not be disturbed by the results. A few will come. Most will not. Sport your color and let my Spirit do his job. Be wise as a fox and gentle as a dove. Let them decide who they will serve. The seekers are being sought and sorted. The sheep from the goats, the wheat from the chafe. They all will know me but all will not choose me. Oh foolish man, how long I have waited. Waiting time is past and harvest time has begun. Time will move very swiftly now as I Am preparing my white horse for the final ride.

Praise you my Lord.

April 25, 2006
What do you have for us that is new
today my Lord?

**Do not be in such a hurry. Moving
my kingdom takes time. You are
always to quick.**

If time is moving swiftly, how can I
not move quickly.

**Again a paradox, when you move
to quickly you slow me down.**

May 4, 2006
Do you have any advice for me
today? I do not recognize my own
needs.

**You have no needs. All your needs
have already been met.**

I know that my needs were met
before the foundation of the earth.
My problem is in receiving what has
already been provided.

**Appreciate what you have and do
not look for things, stuff or**

personal comfort. Look to me in faith believing and all will come as you need it. You do not have a need until you come to the end of self. When you come to the end of self you do not recognize a need because all has already been supplied.

Okay. Help me come to an end of self. I think I have arrived there and loose it the minute I get there.

You will come to the end of self and cross over into another place of being. I will lead you there and be with you always. Here and there. My love, fear not.

Thank you my Lord, I know I can trust in you.

May 10, 2006
What would you like to tell me my Lord?

Breath. Take in my Holy Spirit. Let it nourish your soul and bring healing and health to your body. Relax and release the tension in your body. Focus on me. By my

stripes you are healed. Come away
with me to my quiet place.

CHAPTER 9
I Am the Light and the Way.

Matthew 5:14-16
"You are the light of the world. A
city on a hill cannot be hidden
Neither do people light a lamp and
put it under a bowl. Instead they put
it on its stand, and it gives light to
everyone in the house. In the same
way, let your light shine before men,
that they may see your good deeds
and praise your Father in heaven."

May 18, 2006
Thanks for this sunny day my Lord.
What do you want me to learn
today?

You are my sunshine. You make
me happy. As my light shines
through you, your light shines
back to me.

I know there is more depth to that
statement. Please reveal more to me
by your Holy Spirit.

You are the brightness in my
Glory. When you yield to my light

in you, my light gets brighter. It swells up like the yeast in the bread dough. It makes my Glory more Glorious. My light in you is everlasting. As you have freely received it, so too you must freely give it out. Forever freely receiving and giving. My glorious light is then increased and given back. You cannot out-give me. As you give (light) my abundant light is even more abundant. We both give out and receive back. As the cycle of the sun shines on the earth and draws up the moisture, so it can rain back down. See me in my creation everywhere you look. I Am there in the midst to teach you anew of what has always been. Watch my animals do what they do and just get blessed of me. They do not question me. They just do what they do. They let me do what I do, just bless and provide all of there needs. So just do what you do and let me bless and provide for you. When you struggle, strain and stress you make my job more difficult. It takes me longer to release what you need. Stop it! Stop struggling and make my

**place broader and wider and
deeper and higher than you have
made it in the past. I Am ready to
move. Let me have more space for
my stuff.**

Lord, make my eyes sharper and my
ears clearer. I love you my Lord.

May 26, 2006
Speak to me and increase my
knowledge of you. I want to honor
you.

**I Am not complicated. I do not
bring confusion. Step back away
from problems and you are taking
a step toward Me, the Author of
your comfort in times of trial and
tribulation. I Am, the author of
peace, love, joy and health.**

Thank you for all you are and all you
have done. Teach me how to step
into all you are and stay there.
Onward and upward.

**Step in, I Am holding and
protecting you. Do not fear what
you think the enemy will do to you.
He has no rights when you are in**

my hand. Step in, stand firm in what I have already taught you. Do not move backward. Rest there in me and let my Holy Spirit increase. Give it out when I show you where and when. Just what you know for sure that I have taught you. Your words will be holy and anointed. Anything you know for sure that I have taught you when spoken is anointed. Pray for the ears that will hear. Anointing brings cleansing and growth to those who will hear.

June 5, 2006
I am weary and tired, but I seek your face and want to fulfill your purpose for my life.

When you are weary, it is time to rest. I'll be taking care of things as usual.

What do you do when I am resting?

I Am the manager.

June 16, 2006
Dear Lord Jesus tell me about your love.

My love is higher than the highest mountain. It sits above all that is. It is wider and deeper than the universe. It is incomprehensible. Although I can try to tell you about it, you cannot even understand it. Deeper and higher than anything that can be known of man.

Lord, when I tell you I love you, I feel it is more an act of faith than a true feeling. I am inadequate to love anyone or anything. Why?

Hurts run deep. The scares of which seem to remain forever. I Am the only one that can heal the wounds you bare in your flesh. Turn away from the flesh and seek my face only. You will see it if you seek it. It will come quickly when it comes. Only then will you know love as I Am. It will be balm and ointment to the old wounds. It will then take the scares away. Be honest and true to me and the call on your life. All will come to you as I have promised. I cannot tell a lie. Seek me early and I will be found.

Full of love, comfort and joy.

Thank you my Lord. Help me to seek your face for this is your will for me.

July 1, 2006
There is a lot going on in the world and I do not understand most of it. Help me know my part.

Understanding you need not. Be faithful in your call to praise me. My plan and purposes will be fulfilled on earth as it is in heaven. Pray and praise me only.

Show me more. Give me just a little more of what you know and let me see a little more of what you are doing.

Walk as Abraham walked, full of faith and trust in me. He knew not where he was going, he only knew I made him a promise. You are the same. Trust me and walk forward, one step at a time toward all I have said I would accomplish through you. It will come to pass. Abraham died not seeing his promise. You will not die until

your promise is fulfilled. Fear not,
I Am true to my word. I cannot lie
as it is not in me. I Am love and
truth, pure and holy. I cannot lie.

Why did Abraham not live to see his
promise fulfilled?

It was in the seed that needed to be
planted. You are part of the vine
that comes from the new plant, the
new and grafted branch that will
bear much fruit. I have said it and
it will come to pass. My word is
sure and true. Praise me as I know
exactly what I Am doing. You
cannot know all now or where
would your faith be? You would
not need any. Trust me sweet
daughter, all is coming around.
Full circle is coming. Connect the
line. Stay in step, stay on your
path. Do not stray as I Am coming
soon.

July 31, 2006
Holy Spirit come and teach me
something new I do not know.

Rockets are flying through the air.

Yes, I see some news and I do not understand a lot. You do, so tell me more.

They will fly in all directions to all nations. Ciaos and confusion is coming. Peace and understanding will inhabit my elect. The world will be confounded but, my elect will be at perfect peace. Division has come and multiplication will begin. Consider the cost and pay the price. Treasure is bought without money or gold. Seek me and the higher call. All is well.

August 7, 2006
What did you speak over me before time began? What is my true purpose?

Love me and honor me with your life.

Be more specific. Let me hear the words you spoke for me to be.

My child, my child my beautiful child. You are my design and my creation. You have many facets as I do. Expose them to the light and

each will be revealed.

Show me more, tell me more. You can do this for me. I believe you want me to ask.

Through me you can become like me. See me and all my glory and you can see what you can be. Stay connected to me.

I do know these things. Please show me my strong qualities that you want me to use.

All that is good and holy you may use freely. Freely received, freely give. Back to the garden and my tree of the knowledge of good and evil. Only I can know what is truly good and evil.

Tell me what you spoke over me.

Go forth and multiply after your own kind.

What did you put in me to make me your unique creation? I do know that each one is different and unique.

You have compassion for the weak. I have allowed you to be weak in body so that you can be strong in Spirit.

Do I need to remain weak in body to go forward to be stronger in Spirit?

It is your choice.

I am willing to remain weak in body to know you more. If there is another way, let's take it. I do not particularly like being weak.

August 16, 2006
Where will we go and what will we do Lord Jesus?

Confusion is on its way. We will go in another direction. My Father will show us the way. One day at a time. To look far ahead is unwise. We will go where my Father sends us. He knows best and he knows the way.

Okay, Lord Jesus, I am willing to travel with you. What do I need to take with me?

You need not pack a bag as my Father has a full supply of all that will be needed. He will and has always supplied all our needs. Just be alert and willing and all will fit together.

I think I am ready to go. Do not let me slip away. Keep me in my proper place.

Not to worry. I have my arms around you and I Am not going to let you go. You have made your commitment to me and I have made my commitment to you. Rest in my arms and enjoy the trip.

August 24, 2006
Holy Spirit come and teach me your way.

Light. You are light in me. Light in light, creates glorious light. Light that shines in darkness creates healing to those that see it. I will open the eyes of the blind to see my glorious light. Light will heal from the heart out, until my light shows forth to another. Light to light the pathways of the lost. Light, my

way, for the fallen generations. Forward, move forward; let my light shine from you on the pathway of life everlasting.

Thanks for your light. Help me keep it lit.

It will be kindled by the breath of my Spirit on you and in you. It will not darken or go out. Sometimes fading as in the stress of life, but do not fear as I have my arms around you and you will not fall. Look to me the light to ignite myself in you afresh. Look to me, the faithful one. We will accomplish great and mighty things together.

Thank you my Lord.

August 30, 2006
Teach me more my Lord.

So much to tell you, so much for you to learn and teach. In the beginning God, let us go back to the beginning. To the place of oneness of man and Spirit. That is it. All you need to know will come

from that place. Stay connected and tuned in. You will receive all you need as you need it. Be alert and hear my instructions. Go and do as I tell you. You will not fail, you will prosper. Stay connected and trust in me. We are one-a unit that works together for the divine purpose.

Hold me up and keep me alert and in tune. I know what you require and we both know I am weak. In you I can be strong. Keep me connected for your purpose. I give you permission.

Gentleman that I Am, I will keep you and teach you.

September 17, 2006
What do we need to know as a group?

Join hands together to get the job done. All in one and one in all.

Give us deeper insight.

See me. Keep your eyes on me as you join together. I Am, the leader

of the pack. Follow me. Follow and see what I see, hear what I hear and you will not fail. My body joined together as one, everything fits. Take your place; the table is set and ready to receive you. My guests, the chosen ones, come and dine.

October 5, 2006
Here I am my Lord. Share your knowledge with me that I may bring you glory on earth.

Joy, love, peace and health.

All are yours my Lord. What do I need to know?

I give them all to you along with all else that is mine. All I have belongs to you too. I share freely with those I have chosen. You are indeed among my chosen vessels. You hold all that is inside of you. I will show you when and where to take from this great supply. When, where and who to share it with? Rest and hear me when I speak. I will make it loud enough for you to hear. There will be no doubt. My

power will come and rise up from you to those I will send to you. No need to struggle. Just rest and hear me. I will be there with you to meet with those I will send. I have a plan and it is perfect. You know that what I Am doing is perfect. You have no need to fear. I will be right on time. My words will come forth from you. You need not plan a script. I will supply all you will need. My plan will pop and bloom as the seed comes forth. Fruit of my vine will come to harvest. Watch and see.

October 30, 2006
I'm trying to trust and rest as you have instructed.

Peace, be still my child. I care for you and all your needs. Trust me to know what they are and when you need them. I know all things. All about you, your thoughts, and your desires, trust me to sort out what is important and what you really need.

I can do that, my Lord. Tell me more of what I really need.

You need me to love and comfort you as I need you to love and comfort me.

Do I really know how to love you or anyone else?

Loving is giving of yourself.

Do I?

Yes you do.

CHAPTER 10
Follow Me.

John 10: 3&4
The watchman opens the gate for
him and the sheep listen to his voice.
He calls his own sheep by name and
leads them out. When he has brought
out all his own, he goes on ahead of
them and his sheep follow him
because they know his voice.

November 6, 2006
STOP AND WRITE NOW!
Hush, be still my child. I have
important information for you this
day.

I'm listening, my Lord, what do you
want me to know?

You are mine and I Am yours,
bonded together in love-we are
one.

Lord, you need to hold me close so I
do not stray or wonder from you.

I will do this for you. Do not
worry. Come with me and let me
lead you. We will waltz and glide

together as one unit. I will take you to high and beautiful places you have not been to before this. Just let me lead you. I Am holding you and guiding you on our journey of love bonded together. All is well, all is good, all is working together for your good and my pleasure. I know just how to lead. Relax and mold into my form.

How beautiful my Lord? What a picture of tranquility you have given me. Thank you. Help me to do this. I cannot do this! You need to take control of me and my life. Again, I give you my life for your purpose. Help me to hear, see and obey.

You will not have to obey-just yield to me.

I choose to yield. You have my permission to take control.

Thank you my child.

December 14, 2006
I do not want to be deceived. I want to live in what is truth. Can I be in

this place of power and authority that was given to Jesus? Can I be His body on earth now?

You can be all this and more.

Bring me to where I need to be to receive this and give it out.

You are already there and do not understand or trust it. Be conformed to me. It is not difficult. Do not make it so. Relax and move with me. I will not take you to where you do not belong.

December 26, 2006
What is your Spirit speaking to your Bride?

Get ready. Be prepared. I come quickly now in the twinkling of an eye. When you are not expecting me, we will be together.

Where will we go and what will we do?

We will go to the secret place of the Most High. We will dwell there and honeymoon. We will know

each other and our desires will come to completion. We will then set out on another journey. Old will be passed away and a very new way will begin. Gathering in a different way. You will see and all will be good.

What should I be doing as I wait for this new journey?

Pray and praise my Holy Name. Keep alert and move as I have shown you. You are to represent me as you move. I will be with you to show you how and when. What to do and what to say. As you stay close to me I will be your constant supply. A well that does not run dry. A friend that stickith closer than a brother. We will do everything together.

How is this current call different from the new journey?

Current works take faith. The new journey will not require faith because you will see me as I Am in my fullness. You can partake now but only as I release it. On the new journey all will be shared in my fullness.

I am trying to understand this in my human mind. Is there a better way to understand it?

No, not right now. As I give you faith to believe me now you can only believe what I give you the faith to believe in.

Thank you my Lord. I accept the faith you hold out for me to take. Help me to use it well for your honor and glory.

December 28, 2006
Do you have a special word for me this morning my Lord?

Come out from among them and be separate. As in the threshing floor. Let my Holy Spirit carry you away in the gentle breeze of my Spirit. We will sweep and sway over the earth. Where I go you go, where you go I go. Together bonded in love. The way we move together will be very different from the way the world moves. But

**they (the world) will see and know
who it is that moves differently.
Some will follow and some will see,
yet not follow. Woe be it to them.**

My Lord, only you can keep me as
we sweep and sway. I am willing to
go with you and trust you to keep
me. I know how weak my flesh is.
Help me.

**I will help you and keep you just
because you are willing to come
with me. I have been waiting for
those who will come. I have called
many but I have been able to
choose only a few. Blessings are
upon you and those who are
willing to trust me. I Am-The Most
High God. Keep on believing and
trusting Me. I Am the only one
who knows the way.**

March 18, 2007
Teach me about anointing. I know
your children can have it. How does
it work for your Glory?

**I Am in control of all things and
your destiny. Copycat. Do not be a
copycat because it will not be the**

true image, it will only be a copy. I deal in originals. My copy is unique. It cannot be duplicated. My copy is one of a kind. So do not try to copy someone or even me. I will make the copy I desire and then I will throw away the plan. It is for me only to know all the details and all that has gone into my original. When the anointing falls on you it will burn the exact image I have intended it to be. Do not try to create with false fire. Let me burn through you to create my original and unique design. Praise me for my control and uniqueness. You can only know and see in part. So go along now in confidence that only I Am the one who can burn through you. Do not be afraid of the fire. It will accomplish all I have set it to be.

Thank you my Lord.

Amen-so be it!

About the Author

I was born Elaine Mary Eacobacci in July 1939, the oldest daughter of Veto and Madeline Eacobacci, both second generation Americans. My parents instilled a strong work ethic leading by there own example along with strict moral values. I learned great responsibility at a very early age. At 19 years of age, I married James A. Petersen. We have three sons, Steven, Gary Michael and Scott of whom we are more than proud. Currently, we have two daughters-in-law, Steven's wife, Elizabeth and Scott's wife Ellen. Scott and Ellen have blessed us with four grandchildren, Kelly, Claire, James and Joseph. Gary Michael and his former wife have blessed us with two grandchildren Cassandra and Gary James. We will be celebrating 55 years of marriage in 2013. Life has been most ordinary with our share of ups and downs. I have no clue as to why I have been chosen to share my book with you. May you enjoy it and may the Holy Spirit bless you.

Made in the USA
Coppell, TX
20 January 2021

48505110R00105